THE LIBRARY OF HOLOC

OUT OF THE GHETTO

The Library of Holocaust Testimonies

Editors: Antony Polonsky, Martin Gilbert CBE, Aubrey Newman, Raphael F. Scharf, Ben Helfgott

Under the auspices of the Yad Vashem Committee of the Board of Deputies of British Jews and the Centre for Holocaust Studies, University of Leicester

Out of the Ghetto

JACK KLAJMAN
with Ed Klajman

VALLENTINE MITCHELL
LONDON • PORTLAND, OR

First published in 2000 in Great Britain by
VALLENTINE MITCHELL
Crown House, 47 Chase Side
Southgate, London, N14 5BP

and in the United States of America by
VALLENTINE MITCHELL
c/o ISBS, 5824 N.E. Hassalo Street
Portland, Oregon 97213-3644

Reprinted 2002

Website: http://www.vmbooks.com

British Library Cataloguing in Publication Data
Klajman, Jack
Out of the Ghetto. – (The library of Holocaust testimonies)
1. Holocaust, Jewish (1939–1945) – Poland – Warsaw –
Personal narratives 2. Jews – Poland – Warsaw – Social life
and customs
I. Title II. Klajman, Ed
940.5'318

ISBN 0-85303-389-7
ISSN 1363-3759

Library of Congress Cataloging-in-Publication Data
Klajman, Jack, 1931–
Out of the ghetto / Jack Klajman with Ed. Klajman.
    p. cm. – (The Library of Holocaust testimonies,
ISSN 1363-3759) ISBN 0-85303-389-7 (pbk.)
    1. Klajman, Jack, 1931– 2. Jews–Poland–Warsaw–Biography.
3. Holocaust, Jewish (1939–1945)–Poland–Warsaw–Personal
narratives. 4. Jewish children in the Holocaust–Poland–
Warsaw–Biography. 5. Warsaw (Poland)–History–Warsaw
Ghetto Uprising, 1943. 6. Warsaw (Poland)–Biography.
I. Klajman, Ed. II. Title. III. Series.
DS135.P63 K56 2000
940.53'18'092–dc21
[B]   99-462095

Printed in Great Britain by
The Cromwell Press, Trowbridge, Wiltshire.

Contents

List of Illustrations   vi

The Library of Holocaust Testimonies
by Martin Gilbert   vii

Biographical Note   viii

Introduction   ix

Editor's Note: Historical Background   xi

The Nightmare Begins   1

The Smuggling Life   15

Death   27

The Final Solution   41

The Uprising   61

Three Kilos of Sugar   82

The Catholic Orphan   102

Liberation   121

After the War   136

Epilogue   149

List of Illustrations

Between pages 84 and 85

1. The only remaining photograph of any member of Jankiel's immediate family. His younger brother Eli (left) was killed a few months after this photo was taken in 1943.
2. Jankiel at Three Crosses Square, 1943.
3. Jankiel (right) with his good friend Zybyszek, 1943.
4. Identity card for Jankiel's gentile persona, 'Janek Jankowski', 1944.
5. Mrs Lodzia, Jankiel's guardian angel, 1945.
6. Mrs Lodzia's two daughters, Irka (left) and Marysia, 1945.
7. Jankiel's friend Sevek, having survived the war, taken in 1950.
8. Bull, the leader of the cigarette sellers, 1945.
9. Lutek, the accordian player, 1950.
10. Jankiel in 1945 – he learned to play the accordian in post-war Poland.
11. False identity papers used to get Jankiel out of Poland, 1945.
12. Jankiel, second from the right, with other students at the orphanage in England, 1946.
13. The Head of Jankiel's orphanage in England, 1946.
14. Jankiel (right) with three orphanage colleagues and two dogs; the one on the right is 'Queenie', 1946.
15. Jankiel (Jack) playing the drums after settling in Canada, 1949.
16. Jack's marriage to Sonia in Israel, 1959.

The Library of Holocaust Testimonies

It is greatly to the credit of Frank Cass that this series of survivors' testimonies is being published in Britain. The need for such a series has long been apparent here, where many survivors made their homes.

Since the end of the war in 1945 the terrible events of the Nazi destruction of European Jewry have cast a pall over our time. Six million Jews were murdered within a short period; the few survivors have had to carry in their memories whatever remains of the knowledge of Jewish life in more than a dozen countries, in several thousand towns, in tens of thousands of villages, and in innumerable families. The precious gift of recollection has been the sole memorial for millions of people whose lives were suddenly and brutally cut off.

For many years, individual survivors have published their testimonies. But many more have been reluctant to do so, often because they could not believe that they would find a publisher for their efforts.

In my own work over the past two decades, I have been approached by many survivors who had set down their memories in writing, but who did not know how to have them published. I realized what a considerable emotional strain the writing down of such hellish memories had been. I also realized, as I read many dozens of such accounts, how important each account was, in its own way, in recounting aspects of the story that had not been told before, and adding to our understanding of the wide range of human suffering, struggle and aspiration.

With so many people and so many places involved, including many hundreds of camps, it was inevitable that the historians and students of the Holocaust should find it difficult at times to grasp the scale and range of the events. The publication of memoirs is therefore an indispensable part of the extension of knowledge, and of public awareness of the crimes that had been committed against a whole people.

Martin Gilbert
Merton College, Oxford

Biographical Note

Jack Klajman was born in Warsaw in 1931. He emigrated to England as a refugee in 1945, and moved to Canada in 1948, where he settled in London, Ontario, and worked as a furrier's apprentice. He became a successful small businessman in the community, where he resides today with his wife. They have four children.

Introduction

This book chronicles the story of my experiences in Warsaw during World War II. I have recounted my story to the best of my recollection and in my own words, writing from the perspective of a young child, as I was only eight years old when the war began.

I first thought about writing this book in 1948, and started many drafts over the years. But each time I found that it was too difficult to relive all the painful memories. I would break down in tears as soon as I would get a few lines on paper. This time, perhaps because I am getting on in years, I refused to let any emotions prevent me from writing.

Once I focused on tapping my memory bank, all the experiences came flooding out in great detail. They have been locked away deep in the back of my mind for decades, only surfacing occasionally in the middle of the night when I wake up in a cold sweat because of vivid nightmares in which Germans are trying to kill me. It seems a person can bury the past but cannot get rid of it. For better or worse, your memories are a part of you.

I am proud I have documented my experiences and made my contribution to the historical record. My story is not a happy one, but it is important that I tell it. My wife and four children should know what I saw and lived through. I dedicate this book to them.

I thank my son Ed for his countless hours of writing, editing and researching, which made this book possible.

Editor's Note: Historical Background

Before World War II Warsaw had the largest Jewish community in Europe. In the late 1930s there were nearly 400,000 Jews in the city, making up about one-third of Warsaw's total population. Compared to the Jewish community of Germany, which was predominantly assimilated, Jews in Poland were less integrated with the Catholic majority. Most Warsaw Jews lived in a section of the city called the Northern Quarter. Few gentiles lived there.

Jews had lived in the area since the 1200s, and over the centuries the community developed a strong social, cultural and political identity. However, most Warsaw Jews lived in poverty. The root cause of this was institutionalized anti-Semitism. Discrimination was an open and accepted part of Polish life. Equality for Jews was opposed by almost all Polish political parties and the Catholic Church. Jews were given limited opportunities in society. They could not become doctors or lawyers because the universities would not admit them, and they were barred from public office. Given these limited options, most Jews operated small businesses in the Northern Quarter. Family workshops in trades or crafts were most common.

The situation in Warsaw changed dramatically when the Nazis invaded Poland in September 1939. After annexing Czechoslovakia and Austria in 1938 without the use of force, the Germans showed the world their military strength by demolishing the Polish army in record time. With the permission of the Soviet Union, which was given free rein over the eastern half of Poland, the Germans were governing Warsaw by 1 October 1939.

Because of Hitler's obsessive hatred, Warsaw's Jewish community suffered severe oppression almost immediately. Over time, the persecution became even more extreme. Eventually, the order was given for the 'final solution', and Warsaw's Jews were systematically murdered. Most were sent off to the death camps such as Treblinka. Some died of starvation and disease before they could be gassed, while others were killed by German bullets and artillery. In the end, only a tiny fraction of the original population managed to survive.

Today, there are as few as 5,000 Jews living in Warsaw.

1 • The Nightmare Begins

On 22 April 1931 I was born into a typical Jewish family in Warsaw. My parents had five children. I was the second youngest. My parents named me Jankiel (Jack in English). From the day I was born until the outbreak of the war we lived in a small apartment in the heart of the city's Jewish section – at 14 Wolynska. My father was a tradesman who worked at home.

During the autumn and winter he made fur accessories for cloth-coat manufacturers. In Poland of the 1930s men displayed their affluence and prestige by wearing large outer collars of fur. Women, on the other hand, felt elegant and considered themselves prosperous if they had a mink collar and muff to match. This popularity of fur meant there was plenty of work from garment shops to keep my dad busy through the autumn and winter months. In the spring and summer he converted his fur workshop into a small shoe factory, where he made children's and ladies' sandals. These were then sold to local shoe stores.

While my father was the labourer, my mother was the businesswoman. She would keep the books and take care of all the sales to manufacturers and shopkeepers. She even started up a small retail operation. In the warmer months farmers from the countryside would come to town once a week to sell their produce. My mother would set up a booth at these markets to sell sandals to the farmers. It was always very busy, so I would help her by being on constant guard for potential thieves.

Like most East European Jews we were an extremely close family. I never had any problems with my siblings. Getzel was

1

the oldest – eighteen at the start of the war – while Brenda was two years younger. There was then a gap of five years between her and Menashe, while I was eight and my little brother Eli was six.

My mother once told me I had another brother who was born a year after Brenda, but that he died at the age of one. My mother and father had been invited to an engagement party and left the children with a babysitter. That lady was incompetent, and let the little boy wander around unguarded. He fell and struck his head on the corner of a wooden table. The sitter didn't tell my mother about the incident, thinking it wasn't serious. Later that night, when the boy didn't look well and had a fever, my mother had no idea why. My parents rushed him to the hospital where he died the next day. Apparently, he had suffered a severe concussion that led to some major internal bleeding. The babysitter's carelessness cost the infant his life.

Despite that tragedy, our parents did their best to give us a happy childhood, and we loved and respected them for it. I still remember some of our more enjoyable moments. For instance, I recall that each Passover we would all get new clothes and have a large feast, which considering our lack of wealth was quite an extraordinary thing. In our neighbour-hood, if you were able to eat three meals a day you were considered well off.

Another enduring memory from my childhood involves my mother's intense religious faith. She knew pages of Jewish prayers by heart. In fact, when I was four years old she began educating me in how to read the Talmud. I also remember that while she was extremely knowledgeable about Judaism, she couldn't read or write Polish. She did, however, speak enough of it to get by as a salesperson.

My best friend in my early childhood was a blue-eyed, blond-haired little girl named Irka Ksrigika. She lived just down the street from us at 4 Wolynska – the second last house before Zamenhofa Street. My first memories of Irka are from the age of seven, when we were in first grade at school. In the building where my family lived, many of the adults would get together and stage plays for Saturday afternoon entertainment. Irka and I would dance together at these events to the amusement of all the people in our building.

During the week, I always stopped off at her place so we could walk together to Stafka primary school, which was just around the corner from where we lived. Both Irka and I were at the head of our class – she had the highest grade of the girls while I was first among the boys.

Unfortunately, neither of us was able to experience the second grade at our school.

Our Nazi nightmare began late in the summer of 1939. In August people had been gathering in the streets to talk about what seemed to be an imminent German invasion. Grocery store-owners began to hoard food and charged outrageous amounts for what they made available. People in our neighbourhood were particularly vulnerable to those price increases.

War finally broke out between Germany and Poland on 1 September, and although I was only eight years old at the time it is a day I will never forget.

Late that afternoon, each member of our family was in line at the local bakery. We were preparing for a big family dinner. With food rationing, only one loaf per person was allowed, so each of us had to stand in line to buy a loaf. We had just returned home when we heard planes flying above us. At first we hoped they might be Polish, but that thought didn't last long. Several bombers swooped over our neighbourhood – an area of about 15 condensed blocks. The bombs dropped were devastating, lighting the area up in fire and smoke.

We resided in a two-segment apartment building. Our flat was in the feeble, two-storey segment, which was situated in front of the better-constructed six-storey portion. Two bombs – one of explosive devastation followed by an incendiary fire bomb – landed right on top of the higher, six-storey part of the building. Several people were killed instantly. As fire rapidly spread, we were all in a severe state of shock except for my father, who had been a medic in World War I and knew how to remain calm. He told us that panicking was the worst thing we could do, and that if we kept our cool we would all be OK. He added that we didn't have much time so we all had to listen very carefully to his instructions.

The plan, he said, was for all of us to meet at Uncle Chaim's place. My uncle lived with his family at 48 Pawia, several blocks away from us. Looking out the window, my dad had quickly surveyed the damage in the area and figured Uncle Chaim's building was in a part of the neighbourhood that had not been hit. If he was wrong about that our orders were to go to Uncle Jankiel's, who lived even further away from us.

My dad told my sister Brenda to grab my hand and for the two of us to leave first. He said we were not to separate under any circumstances. As Brenda and I scrambled out the door I heard my father yell out 'God be with you'.

Out in the streets, tenants of several bombed high-rise dwellings in the area were running around in a state of panic. German planes were diving down strafing people with their machine guns. They killed anyone in sight – men, women and children. We ran carefully from house to house, dodging the Luftwaffe's bombs and gunfire.

Our neighbourhood was a huge inferno, with flames leaping from many buildings. And once the fire had burned all it could, what was left came crashing to the ground. Meanwhile, the German planes kept coming and coming. Just when one squadron would fly off and it looked as if it was all over, another would come in and continue to pound us.

We just kept running and tried to block out all the chaos.

4

My sister stayed in control by repeatedly saying 'God is with us. We will make it Jankiel, we will make it'. But those words didn't stop me from wondering about what had happened to my parents. And if they were dead, I asked myself without letting Brenda know I was thinking it, what would happen to us?

It took about an hour and a half, but we were lucky enough to make it to my uncle's place. My sister and I embraced in each other's arms once we entered the apartment building. The bombing had quieted down somewhat, and it seemed that my uncle's area of the Jewish Quarter had not been hit.

Tears of joy and sorrow trickled down my cheeks. I was elated that we had survived, but gravely concerned that no one else from our family had arrived yet. But Brenda held firmly to her faith that all would be well. 'Don't cry Jankiel. You'll see, they will soon be here', she said, hugging me tightly. 'Just wait and see, they'll be here soon.' We passed the time by describing to Uncle Chaim and Auntie Sarah how our place had been burned to the ground and how much of our street was ablaze. About 30 minutes after we got there, the rest of the family arrived. We all hugged each other and thanked God that He had guided us safely to the apartment.

The ecstasy of seeing everyone again, however, soon wore off. They hadn't brought anything with them – not even the seven loaves of bread for which we had stood in line for hours. All we had literally were the clothes on our backs. Fortunately, Uncle Chaim and Auntie Sarah had some food and were willing to share it with us.

Like my father, my uncle was a poor tradesman who made fur collars for the clothing trade. He had 12 children – six boys and six girls. I vividly remember how my mother used to prepare and deliver food parcels for them. While our family incomes were comparable, my parents were better off because they had only five children at home. I know we could have used the extra food, but my mother was an extremely kindhearted and charitable woman. I remember she used to say to us that God would reward us for taking care of others in need. 'If we're capable, we have to help them,' she would say. 'Give and thou shalt receive in return.'

My mother considered her mother to be the role model for all of us to follow. I remember being told that when my mother was four years old, her father died prematurely from some kind of illness, and that her mother was left alone to raise her three children. She then bought a piece of land 20 miles outside of Warsaw where she ran a farm, and had an orchard for growing apples, pears and cherries.

Grandma used to refer to herself as a city girl turned farmer. 'The fresh air and the healthy fruit and vegetables will keep you alive until 100,' she would say. In her seventies she still loved to live and work at the farm. Above all, I remember that she was very generous. She would ride in on her horse-and-buggy, bringing us bags full of potatoes, turnips and cabbages, which we could store for the winter.

Soon after World War II came to Poland, my grandmother lost both her orchard and her farm when they were expropriated. Unfortunately, we understood how she felt. Because of the bombing, we had lost everything too. That included my father's equipment – and operating those machines was all he knew. We had no idea what he would do for a living without them.

For the moment though our immediate concern was trying to survive as we stayed with Uncle Chaim. Their place was small and crowded: fourteen of them already lived uncomfortably by having to share only two rooms, one of which was a kitchen. With seven more people, there were now 21 bodies crammed into the apartment. Things could have been worse, however, had more relatives turned up. My father had five brothers and five sisters, and all had children.

My dad realized how difficult it would be to stay with so many people in such a small place, and he told us that the following morning we would try to make it to Uncle Jankiel's. He and his wife Hanna were my favourites. They were the most affluent of all my aunts and uncles, and whenever they used to visit they would bring some kind of treat. Like my father, Uncle Jankiel made shoes, but he had a larger operation than my dad, and he had only three children to take care of, which was considered a small family at that time. They lived in a four-room apartment, which included a cellar that was used as a workshop for shoe-making. Our hope was that they would let us stay in the cellar.

We were physically and emotionally exhausted from the ordeal of the day, so we had no problem falling asleep that night as we crammed together for the night on Uncle Chaim's apartment floor. The bombing started again the next day so we had to postpone our move to Uncle Jankiel's by 24 hours. As the bombing subsided somewhat on the third day, we bade tearful farewells to Uncle Chaim and his family and made it over to Uncle Jankiel's, where he promptly took us to the basement. In fact, his family had already moved there. Under the constant threat of bombing, the basement was much safer than his above-ground flat. As we expected, they were very generous towards us. They shared all their food with us and sacrificed their furniture as firewood for cooking and heat.

The next day my oldest brother Getzel ventured back to our old home to survey the damage and see if he could collect anything. He found the place had been totally obliterated; only the foundations remained. He returned with tears in his eyes. 'It's all gone Mom', he said as he hugged my mother. 'Everything's gone. But at least we are all alive and that means everything', he added as they started to cry. It was so strange to see Getzel, who was my idol, cry. He was an excellent soccer goalie, and I used to love to watch him play in matches. He was also a great dancer and very popular with girls. He was just a fun-loving young man who, despite our upbringing, did not have any interest in religion, though he used to go through the motions and say prayers with us each day to please my mother.

We all had tears in our eyes as we realized that all the material remnants of our past had been destroyed. My mother was extremely distressed, noting that not even a single photograph had been saved. My sister then hugged my mother and, through her own tears, offered a typical dose of optimism. 'When peace sets in, we will make it back again,' she said. 'We will build it all up again. We will be able to get other pieces of furniture and clothing.'

Warsaw was under siege for the rest of the month. The German attack was particularly vicious on 13 September, which was the eve of Rosh Hashanah – the Jewish New Year. On that day, artillery fire accompanied heavy aerial bombardments, and Warsaw lay in ruins. Yet the Germans continued to bomb the city. In fact, towards the end of September, they intensified their efforts.

Throughout September there was no gas, heat or running water. Getting adequate food and water was no easy task. Residents had to reach the Vistula River for water, or crowd around bomb craters which filled with rain. We were lucky to be living only two blocks away from the Vistula, so for us water was not a major issue.

As for food, we shared in my uncle's supplies, which didn't last long. Meanwhile, most stores had been destroyed in the bombings, and all the food had disappeared from the shelves earlier in the month anyway. To eat, you had to be enterprising. People killed their pets for the meat; and others looked for stray animals in the streets.

One day Getzel heard that a pickling plant was on fire and despite the dangers of the streets, waded through the war zone to get to the facility. He returned with two large containers of pickles. Getzel risked his life for the meal, but soon after eating all the pickles, we realized fasting that night would have been better than ingesting those things. They were spoiled and rotten, and we all ended up with severe stomach cramps.

Another time we heard there was a ship in the harbour that had caught fire. Its cargo was said to contain rice. Risking his life yet again, Getzel trekked to the ship, filled a large pillow-case with rice, and returned safely. Many others didn't return. They were engulfed by the fire or killed by falling debris. That rice became our mainstay for several days. We cooked it over an open fire, breaking furniture into small pieces to use as precious firewood.

One of the best meals we had came after a Polish army horse was killed by shrapnel on the street in front of our building. My father was one of many men who rushed out to carve up a piece of the dead animal. He brought back a large chunk and what with that and the rice, we had a virtual feast on our hands.

In the short term we survived, but knew we couldn't live in that manner for ever. And we figured it wouldn't be long before Warsaw would fall to the Germans and Poland would capitulate. Everyone knew that the Polish army, which still had only a cavalry of horses in many places, was no match for the well-mechanized strength of the German army. Poland had no choice but to give up unconditionally. On 27 September, the country surrendered.

Warsaw was a disaster area. Fires were still raging and buildings had been flattened. People were in a state of shock and disbelief as September had been a month of nothing but death and destruction.

Within a few days, the Germans were to arrive. We figured that in time they would rebuild Warsaw and the city would survive. But as Jews, we were worried about our future. We had heard what the Germans had done to Jews in their country – the harassment, the vandalism and the violence. Even so, we had no idea how bad it would get.

The German army, with all its might of tanks and trucks, rolled into Warsaw on 1 October 1939. I vividly remember how the very tall men in their fancy uniforms and high leather boots marched in as if they were great heroes. It was a large, colourful parade, complete with loud bands playing. The Nazis projected an image of invincibility – that they would take over the world and would have very little difficulty in doing so.

Days after taking control, the Germans began a reign of tyranny against the Jews, and they had support in their efforts from many Poles who were anti-Semitic. With the city in shambles, the conquerors established bread lines to feed the masses. Poles and Jews were fed separately, with the Jews getting far less. As a result, many Jews joined Polish lines. Some Poles who didn't know any German quickly learned how to say '*Ein Jude*' in order to identify Jews. Often to a chorus of laughter, the young German soldiers would pull the Jew aside and beat him senseless.

On a few occasions the Nazis set up soup kitchens on Moronwoska Street to show the world how they cared for the Jews. The conquerors filmed themselves in the Jewish section, distributing a rich, meaty soup with fresh bread. It was all such transparent propaganda. I remember everyone in my family got diarrhoea on those few occasions when we were given that fat soup. Our bodies couldn't cope after having eaten so little for several weeks.

What their movies didn't show was the Nazis confiscating Jewish property, and enacting a series of increasingly harsh decrees. To start with, Jews had to turn over all their gold, silver and jewellery. While not everyone followed the rule, you were in big trouble if you were caught withholding the valuables. Jews were also rounded up for forced labour, and

10

treated brutally in the process. The Nazis would take women, for instance, and force them to clean toilets using their underwear as cleaning rags. Meanwhile, old Orthodox men who just happened to be walking down the street would have their beards chopped off and then were savagely beaten.

On top of this, many Poles would conduct pogroms against the Jews, much to the pleasure of the Germans. This terror was made more convenient in November when the Germans decreed that all Jews over the age of ten were to wear blue armbands displaying the Star of David. Facing such a frightening climate of hostility, most Jews were scared even to leave their apartments.

As for my family, we knew we were being an unfair burden on Uncle Jankiel, so we left his home soon after the Germans arrived. Because we couldn't afford rent anywhere, we went back to our old building. It was just a burned-out shell of a structure and, with nothing remaining of our apartment, we made our way down to the cellar. There was a small room down there which became our temporary home until we could accumulate some money. There was no heating and no floor – just black soil. We laid some boards down and covered them with blankets, which Uncle Jankiel had given us. Staying there was very dangerous. The whole building could have collapsed on top of us at any time. But it was the only free accommodation we could think of, so we had no choice in the matter.

My mother managed to scrounge some money and belongings from her relatives, and that got us started on the road to recovery. She would sell the items on the street markets, which were the dominant form of commerce in the Jewish area. The shops never recovered from all the damage they had sustained, and prices had become so expensive that haggling on the street was the only practical way the community could function. By the end of November, the sidewalks were filled with people bartering for the necessities of life.

Eventually, my mother made enough zlotys from shrewd buying and selling to get us into a little place in the ghetto at 64 Mila. Like our original home, it had one large room with a kitchen. My sister slept in the kitchen, while the rest of us shared the other room.

As for my father, he became seriously ill before the end of the year with a kidney disease. We could not afford any medicine – not that there was any available – but he managed slowly to recover. Unfortunately though, even when he felt well physically, he was struggling mentally and emotionally because he couldn't work at his trade. He had no equipment and, with the extreme poverty that had set in, he had few potential customers. In time, his depression led to renewed deterioration of his physical condition, and he became increasingly weak and vulnerable.

With my father unable to cope, my oldest brother Getzel had to take on more responsibility for supporting the family. And he did his best until one day in early 1940 he was plucked off the street by the Germans, pushed into a truck, and forced to remove snow from the streets. At the end of the day, some of these workers were sent to labour camps. Getzel was among the fortunate sent home, but the experience had a profound impact on him.

When he came back, his first words were: 'Mom and dad, I'm leaving tomorrow for Russia.' He said lots of people were doing it every day. The border was still open at that time, and remained so until Germany declared war on the Soviet Union. He explained to my parents that he was going with his friend Herschel. Herschel was not just any friend – he was Brenda's boyfriend. In fact, they were even talking about marriage at the time.

Both Getzel and Herschel wanted to take Brenda with them, pleading with my mother that they would take good care of her. My sister desperately wanted to go with them, but my mother wouldn't allow it. She said Getzel and Herschel were older than Brenda, and being men they would be able to handle the rough journey. She insisted it would be too difficult for Brenda. My mother also argued it was bad enough that she had to lose her first-born; she said two children leaving the family was too much. However, she did offer a compromise to keep Brenda happy. Getzel and Herschel were to report back on their status, and when my mother was satisfied that all was well for them in Russia, we would make every effort to move east and join them.

Very early the next day Getzel threw a few things in a bag and my mother gave him what money she could spare. There were lots of hugs, kisses and tears as he left. It was a very sad day for all of us.

About a week passed before we received a letter from Bialystock, a Polish city on the Russian border. Getzel wrote to say that he had applied for a work visa at the Soviet consulate in Bialystock. He made it clear that he didn't care where he would live in Russia – he just wanted to stay away from Poland. He also mentioned that my mother was wise not to send Brenda because the waiting compound was disgusting. Lice were everywhere, there were no facilities to bathe or do laundry, and people had to sleep on a dirt floor.

The next letter we received came from Russia. Getzel had finally acquired a Soviet visa. Like most people who fled Poland, he had been sent to the Ural Mountain area of Siberia, and was assigned work as a bricklayer. He wrote regularly from his address at 'Gorod Berezniki, Molotonskaja Oblonsk', an address that has been firmly planted in my memory since the first time I saw it on an envelope. Judging by his letters he seemed to be doing fine. He wrote that he was treated well at his job and enjoyed studying Russian in the evenings. I also remember that he enclosed photos of himself taken on construction sites with some of his new

Russian friends dressed in their big puffy jackets as they braved the -40°C cold.

As for Herschel, he got approval to enter into Russia a week or two after Getzel. However, instead of going to Siberia as instructed, he told the Soviets he'd rather stay near the border so he'd be relatively close to Brenda. This did not please the authorities. Like many others who voiced their preferences, Herschel was considered a traitor, and as punishment was sent to a labour camp. While that may seem cruel, it was much better than being sent back to Poland. Returning into the hands of the Nazis would have meant certain death. At least in the labour camps there was a good chance of survival. At the end of the war, many of the prisoners were able to come back to Poland to search for survivors, though I don't know what happened to the man who might have become my brother-in-law.

Getzel had applied for papers to bring all of us to Russia, but he warned that it would take some time to work through the bureaucracy. I remember my mother crying the day she received that letter from Getzel. She cried partly for joy, that one day we'd be able to move to Russia, and partly out of sorrow as she thought about abandoning her mother, who at eighty was too old to be accepted by the Russians. She also worried about all her relatives, and all the other Jews in Poland who would have to live under Nazi occupation.

Unfortunately, we never had the chance to leave anyone behind. When war broke out between the Soviet Union and Germany in June 1941, we lost contact with my brother and never heard from him again. To this day, I do not know what happened to him. Maybe he was conscripted into the army and killed in battle. Whatever his fate, I know it was better than what was to come for the rest of us in Poland.

2 • *The Smuggling Life*

Life became increasingly difficult under German rule in the cold winter months of early 1940 and, without Getzel to help, I began working the streets to try to get food for my family. Using skills I had learned from watching my mother, I took several small items from our apartment and sold them on the city's street markets. With that money I bought cigarettes, which I offered to farmers who had set up stalls in the markets. I knew that most of these men were smokers, but were unable to leave their stalls so they would pay extra for the delivered cigarettes.

I would get up at 5 a.m., when my mother would make a breakfast of potato soup for me. Then I was off. Because we didn't have enough money for leather, I wore wooden shoes, which gave no protection from the -20°C temperature. Most people got by on bare feet, even in the snow. I was one of the lucky ones who had wooden shoes. I just had to do my best to block out the cold as I went to the corner of Lubetska and Mila, where I bought a load of 'Junakies' cigarettes – the cheapest available. By 9 or 10 a.m., I had usually sold about 200 of them. That earned me enough of a profit to purchase a 1 kilo loaf of rye bread and a couple of potatoes. I was very proud of myself each day I brought that food home, and I knew my parents were proud of me too.

My contribution was extremely important, but it took more than just my efforts to feed the family. My older brother Menashe also sold cigarettes, operating a few blocks away from me so we wouldn't compete with one another. My mother and sister also helped out by selling small items at the Warsaw Bazaar on Smochia Street.

We probably wouldn't have survived had we not gathered

all that extra food on our own. Rations were supplied to the Jews, but these weren't enough to survive on, and by early 1940 you started to see the suffering resulting from malnutrition. Then the situation rapidly worsened. The Germans wanted Jews from in and around Warsaw concentrated in the Jewish Quarter. So the population density increased daily, to the point where 30 per cent of Warsaw's people were crammed into 5 per cent of the city's area.

Meanwhile, less and less food was made available, and disease began to take its toll. With the Germans progressively reducing the water supply, proper sanitation was an impossibility and lice became ubiquitous. Soon after, outbreaks of typhoid, tuberculosis and diphtheria became major problems. It was just what the Germans wanted, giving them the opportunity to post signs designating the Jewish area as a 'plague-infested' zone to be avoided.

In the second half of 1940 German plans for the Warsaw Ghetto came into focus. In August they announced that there were to be three zones – German, Polish and Jewish – with the Jews not allowed to enter into German territory. Then in October it was announced that the Jews were to be contained by brick walls.

By the end of November, construction of the enclosure was complete. The ghetto walls were about 10 feet high, up to 20 feet in places, and topped with crushed glass. There were German and/or Polish guards at all the entrances, and only those few Jews with the appropriate work permits were permitted to leave, while Poles were forbidden from entering. The ghetto area of some 15–20 square blocks was completely cut off from the rest of the city.

The situation was desperate before the walls were erected, but the conditions became even harsher by early 1941. Malnutrition was replaced by mass starvation. By early 1941 it was common to see men, women and especially children dying in the streets. Corpses were dragged off the pavements for mass burials of 50 at a time. When someone died, others stole the clothes off his or her body. The corpse was then covered with newspapers until the collecting wagons came along. Eventually, people became so blasé about death that no one even bothered to cover the bodies anymore.

Under such duress, many who didn't die of starvation or disease saw only a grim future and withered away with broken hearts. The ghetto was so bad you couldn't even get any fresh air because there were no trees; the boundaries of the ghetto excluded all parks and playgrounds. It was just one big mass of human misery and suffering.

For my family and me, life also went from bad to worse. Before the walls were erected we were effectively able to acquire food, but once the walls went up they isolated us from our food source. Officially, the rule in January 1941 was that any adult Jew caught on the Aryan side received a 1,000 zloty fine and three months in jail. Towards the end of the year the penalty changed to the death sentence. Although the law was more lenient for children, the reality was that the wall was patrolled by men with guns who were free to shoot you and/or severely beat you – whatever your age.

Closed off from the outside world, most children took to the ghetto streets and begged for food. But there were thousands of children and precious little food. I realized this tactic was sure to lead to starvation, and that there was only one solution. Somehow, I had to leave the ghetto to get food.

My first foray outside the ghetto involved a friend of mine named Sevek, a brash boy about four years older than me. He lived in our building, and our families knew each other quite well. Sevek and I agreed to establish a business partnership in which we would smuggle food into the ghetto. I'm certain we were among the first Warsaw Ghetto smugglers.

Sevek had some money, which we used to get ourselves

started. We found a hole in the wall, and slipped into the Aryan section. We used his money to buy food – bread, marmalade, sausage and other essentials. We took it all back wrapped in bedspreads and pillowcases, which meant our return to the ghetto was even riskier than our exit. Fortunately, we weren't caught.

After providing our parents with enough food for our families, we then offered the rest to ghetto Jews in exchange for valuables such as watches or jewellery. We took those items back over to the Aryan side and sold them for a good sum of money, which we used to get more food. This cycle went on for a couple of trips. We ended the day with a good profit.

I had thought Sevek and I agreed to be equal partners, but after that successful first day of working together he kept 75 per cent for himself and refused to consider giving me more. As I result, I broke off our partnership and the next day tried to operate alone. To get myself started, I asked my sister if she could part with her one and only fancy dress. I knew it could sell for enough money to kick-start my scheme. She wasn't happy to turn it over to me, but in a typical display of kindness, she gave it to me and wished me luck.

Within a few trips I had my family fed, and could start thinking of making a small profit. I was particularly proud that I was doing better than Sevek. By the time I completed two or three trips, he was just finishing his first.

In time, more and more children started to smuggle, although we were never more than a select minority. We were very resourceful, using whatever means available to get out of the ghetto. Being children, we were small – often able to get through holes in the wall that adults made for us. Or we could break through ourselves – chipping away one brick at a time. Eventually, you could make a big enough hole to just squeeze through. Often, the German guards and Polish police would find our holes and fill them in, so we would always be looking to punch out new ones to stay one step ahead of them.

When it wasn't possible to go through the wall we went over it. This was the more difficult way because you had to scale all the brick and then manoeuvre across the crushed glass cemented at the top. To protect our skin, we put some thick rags over the glass so we could stay at the top for a few moments before jumping down. Even after getting to the other side you were only partway to safety. With guards buzzing around the wall and all its entrances there was no assurance that you would get by undetected.

This dangerous, hustling lifestyle quickly came to dominate my childhood. It was depressing to realize that other children were playing with toys while I was risking my life to feed my family. My only breaks came on the weekends. I would not smuggle on Saturdays, the Jewish Sabbath, or Sundays when all the stores were closed on the Aryan side.

My older brother Menashe did his best to smuggle too. Unfortunately, he was never comfortable with the task. He had a quiet, passive personality – similar to my father's. He loved to sing and paint. If the war had not destroyed our lives, I think my parents would have tried to save their money to send him to Paris to go to art school. I don't think he ever would have been much of a businessman. As for my mother and my sister, they were busy taking care of my father. As conditions in the ghetto worsened, he was getting weaker by the day.

Sometimes when I smuggled it was too risky to return and I had to stay on the Aryan side overnight. That could be a dangerous situation, but fortunately I became friendly with a Polish couple who were prepared to help me. Mr and Mrs Slawcia were a middle-aged couple who did not have any children of their own. They knew I was Jewish but always gave me strong support. They let me stay with them when I couldn't get back to the ghetto – which was especially important on the bitterly cold days of winter.

The couple owned a café on Grochowska Street in Praga.

Their shop was small – only four tables – but it was always full, so they managed to earn a decent living. I would often bring them some small items from my bartering, and in return they would feed me their speciality – sausage and sauerkraut. In addition, they distilled whiskey in their home. When I would drink it my tongue would go numb from its potency. But I didn't let that deter me. I felt I was enduring the hardships of an adult, so I was entitled to behave like one.

Most of my excursions to the Aryan side went well, though I was caught several times. On a few occasions, the policemen gave me a painful beating with their hard rubber sticks. As well, they would confiscate all the goods I had accumulated. To protect myself from being put in jail, I used Eli's identity papers to show that I was only eight years of age, which is about how old I looked. They'd see those papers and release me to my sister with a warning not to do it again.

The documents helped but they guaranteed nothing. One day a Polish policeman caught me on the Aryan side and I was taken to a jail. They didn't even bother to look at my papers. Fortunately, it was assumed that I was just a Polish youth who was stealing some small goods. Not long before that I had bought a cross which I wore around my neck to protect my identity.

I was also helped by not having a Jewish appearance. I had a small nose, kept my hair short, and spoke fluent Polish. So it was natural for them to assume I was Polish, and I wasn't going to argue. I just told them that I was an eight-year-old from outside Warsaw, and that I was deeply sorry for being a trouble-maker.

While processing the paperwork for my release, they put me in a room with a 12-year-old boy. The security was not particularly tight as our second-floor cell had a regular glass window without any bars. The boy I was with said he had been caught before, so he expected soon to be taken away to a more secure jail. He decided that if he ever was to escape, he would have to do it from our holding cell. He smashed the window and jumped to the ground. That was as far as he got. I think he broke both his legs when he hit the ground, and the authorities did not look pleased when they took him away, possibly to be shot. Soon after he jumped I was released. I knew if I was caught a second time, they would not be as lenient with me, a fact that they reminded me of on my way out.

The scariest moment I ever had crossing the wall came at the hands of a vicious German major we called Frankenstein. Around the middle of 1941 he was assigned patrol duty of the Stawka wall, with his home station at the gate on the corner of Zelazna and Leszno Streets.

Frankenstein was a short, bull-legged, creepy-looking man. He loved to hunt, but I suppose he must have become bored with animals and decided that shooting Jewish children was a more enjoyable pastime. The younger the children, the more he enjoyed shooting them. He killed and injured so many that it became necessary to open a surgical emergency clinic in my former school, which was in his patrolling vicinity.

He guarded the area in a jeep with a mounted machine gun. As children would climb the wall, Frankenstein and a German assistant would zoom in from out of nowhere on their killing machine. The other man always drove so Frankenstein had quick access to his machine gun.

Once you were spotted there was no time to hide – it didn't matter whether you were in the process of climbing or just near the wall and getting ready. It took him only seconds from the time he eyed you until the moment he murdered you with a spray of bullets.

Often, when there were no climbers to kill, he would summon ghetto kids who just happened to be in his line of sight – a long way from the wall and with no intention of going anywhere. Typically, he would just yell out 'Jude', and you knew that was it. Your life was over. After you walked towards him, he would yell at you for a moment and then say you were free to leave. Moments later, he would pull out his pistol and shoot you in the back of the head. After his successful hunt, he'd walk back to his jeep and drive off until the next time – and no one knew when or where that would be. If you were a smuggler, you were terrified of him. But you had no choice. You had to eat.

One day I was approaching the Stawka wall with a bag full of food I was bringing back from the gentile market. While I was standing still, scouting around before I neared the wall, Frankenstein drove speedily towards the wall – firing his gun to get my attention.

He pulled up in front of me and yelled for me to walk towards him. A numb feeling gripped my body. I knew right there and then that my life was over. He was going to kill me, probably with a bullet to the head. In my heart, I wanted it to be over as quickly as possible. I hated his guts and visualized myself spitting in his face before he killed me. Fortunately, I restrained myself from doing that. Otherwise, I wouldn't be here to write this story.

Buoyed by the adrenaline rush of impending death, words started pouring out of my mouth in a desperate attempt to save my skin. I was actually trying to convince the cold-blooded monster that he was making a mistake. 'I don't understand what you are saying,' I pleaded. 'I am a Catholic boy', I cried, helped by the fact that I was wearing a cross around my neck.

'I'm just trying to make a few zlotys for my poor parents. Father is sick with a heart condition. I need to make a little money to put some food on our table.' My whole spiel was in Polish, and the German Frankenstein couldn't understand a word of it. I kept rambling at him as he carried on a discussion with his assistant.

I had the feeling Frankenstein's partner was a Pole with German heritage who was from somewhere near the German border. He seemed to understand my Polish. He intently looked at me when I spoke and was fixated on the cross I wore around my neck.

It was a pathetic scene, but the pleading was my only chance. Showing off the cross hanging from my neck, I started to recite all the Catholic prayers I knew. I figured that if I could plant a seed of doubt in their minds, they might think I really was a gentile. I begged incessantly, crying out for them to believe me. I promised that I would never again come to the ghetto and deal with the Jews. With a bag full of smuggled goods in hand, I could tell I didn't fully convince them, but thanks to the cross, the assistant wasn't entirely convinced I was Jewish either.

That Pole had lobbied on my behalf, but my fate was still in Frankenstein's hands. They talked it over for a few moments – the Polish man doing most of the talking, gesturing with his hands. Frankenstein was tapping his fully drawn gun in his palm, probably salivating about the prospect of blowing my brains out.

When they stopped talking, they came closer to me. Frankenstein just stood there staring down at me – mumbling something that I couldn't understand. A moment later, he motioned for me to walk away.

I figured that the next event was a bullet in the back of my head. That made me even more desperate. To his surprise, I raced towards him, grabbed his pant leg and knelt down on one knee. Pretending to be a Catholic preparing for death, I raised my hand and traced a cross on my chest.

He was unfazed. He still had his gun in hand ready to shoot me. I got up to take the final few paces of my life, but walked backwards very slowly so we faced one another. If he was to kill me he would have to do it on my terms, not in his cowardly way. Shockingly, he didn't shoot. Instead, he ran over and he gave me a kick in the butt with his huge, heavy boots. He packed his gun away and yelled at me to get lost. They got back in the jeep and drove off; he really was letting me go.

I was incredibly lucky. If Frankenstein's partner hadn't happened to have been a Pole, I don't think I would have survived. As happened so many times in the war, I may have been in the wrong place, but I was lucky to be caught there at the right time.

The instantaneous high of dodging death momentarily drowned out the agonizing pain of Frankenstein's forceful kick as I ran to a nearby building. A group of people had gathered from a second-storey window to watch the incident unfold. Crying with joy, they ran up and started kissing me.

'We expected to be burying you, not talking to you,' one of them said, not believing what she had just seen. 'He let you go with just a kick in the ass? What did you say to him that he let you live? Tell us, tell us. No one has ever escaped him before.' Said another: 'My boy, you have just been reborn. You have just escaped the devil himself. If he did not take your life, it means God is good to you. He wants you to live. You are going to survive the war. Yes, you will survive the war. If you can make it past him, you can make it past anyone.'

I couldn't believe what had happened. I literally pinched myself to make sure it was real. It's still hard to believe I survived that episode. For a few days after the event, word got around about what had happened. It seemed everyone in the ghetto knew about it.

I was thrilled at my good fortune but at the same time the whole incident left me severely traumatized. I felt like a walking ghost, knowing that I really should have been dead. Emotionally, I never fully recovered from that incident and it took several days and several nightmares before I even became functional again. On top of that, he had kicked me so hard that for days I could barely walk.

Even after the terror of Frankenstein, I had no choice but to go back to smuggling. I hated doing it, but I simply had no choice. I just blocked out the fear as best I could and day after day forced myself to go. Hunger forces you to take risks. How was my family going to eat if I didn't smuggle?

That is not to say that I didn't have moments when I nearly gave up. Once I was caught and found myself in the Gestapo headquarters being interrogated. They weren't fooling around, and I was sure I was dead. Just the way they stared at me made sweat pour down my forehead.

With the cross around my neck, I pretended I was a gentile child when they interrogated me. But I was also prepared to give in if it came to that. The anguish was beginning to be too much, and I thought life could mercifully end if I gave up. However, I can honestly say I heard little voices in my head telling me not to surrender – to stick to my story.

As two men came over to interrogate me, I kissed my cross and said a prayer loudly in Polish. I told them I was only smuggling to support my poor Polish family and that I would never again do it. I begged them to release me because my family would be getting worried if I didn't return soon. After 30 minutes they told me I'd be let go as long as I promised never to return to the ghetto again, and they told me to tell my father to get a job so I wouldn't put myself at risk again.

I thanked them, promised I wouldn't do it again, and ran off free as a bird. Once again, I couldn't believe my good fortune to be in the clutches of the Germans and then escape. As I walked away, I kept thinking of the little voices I heard telling me not to give up. I inhaled a few breaths of delicious fresh air and dashed home.

In many respects, I admit I often had more guts than brains during those smuggling days. A lot of luck didn't hurt either. When I got caught a couple more times after that incident, I fed them my standard story of being a gentile boy trying to earn a few bucks. Each time, they just told me to go back home and never come into the ghetto again. I thanked them in Polish, crossed my heart, and left by saying: 'Thank you Jesus for guiding me.'

Since I was fortunate to be caught by different men on each of those occasions, I got away with little more than a scolding. Perhaps the jails became overcrowded, or it was my appearance, or maybe it was because I was handled by soft, lazy or stupid people, but whatever the reason, I managed to slip through the cracks of the system. Somehow they believed my story – they didn't take me back to the Gestapo headquarters where all they had to do was take my pants down to reveal my circumcised penis.

The smuggling lifestyle and virtual hand-to-mouth existence I had to endure for so long gave me a pretty cynical view of the world during the crucial, formative years of childhood. Yet no matter how bad conditions became, my family and I never lost hope. We thought one day the Germans would be defeated and life would return to normal. Until then, our approach was to live for the moment, hoping to be around the next hour and the next day, and hoping that soon life would get better. You truly had to believe that. Survival is impossible without hope, even if it is false hope.

3 • Death

The contrast between the ghetto and the outside world was chilling. The Aryan side seemed like heaven. People were working and food was plentiful. Conditions were more difficult than usual, but there still was a sense of normality.

Inside the ghetto, there was nothing but misery. Each time I returned, my first sight was countless tiny, starving children begging for scraps of food. Many didn't even look like human beings any more. They were at death's door, either so seriously malnourished that their bellies were distended like giant balloons, or so thin that they were nothing more than skin-and-bone zombies. I always tore one of my loaves of bread into small bits and placed them in the skinny little hands of some of these children. It was heartbreaking to see such a pathetic sight. Each day I arrived home with tears in my eyes.

With scores of people dying daily under the inhuman conditions of the ghetto, it was only a matter of time before someone in my family would succumb. Already in a weakened physical and mental state, my father was the first to go. Not long after becoming very ill – and only months after the ghetto was established – he died battling a mysterious disease my mother refused to talk about. As I reflect back on his symptoms all I remember is that the problem involved his kidneys.

My father stood about six feet two inches tall, weighed about 200 pounds and was a very handsome man with lots of curly hair. At least that's the image I remember of him – not what he looked like when he died, which bore no resemblance to his appearance from before the war.

As we became poorer and poorer, my father started to become more and more depressed. All he knew was how to make fur accessories and sandals. Failing that, he had no other means to support the family. He had to watch me take to the streets early each morning – sitting idly by as though I was the father and he the child. For a man who had always worked hard to sustain his family, it was a dreadful thing to have to go through. This helplessness fuelled his poor health. He was so ill he always slept on the only bed in our cramped apartment.

My father's plight was typical of what happened to most adults in the ghetto. The only ones who had any chance to survive were the street-savvy, rough, tough deal-makers. My lifestyle had brought me into contact with these big-time smugglers. They would bribe guards to bring wagons of stuff into the ghetto. I admit they had a certain callousness to ignore all the misery of fellow Jews, but I admired these gangster-like figures. They were just doing what was necessary to survive. I became a friend to a number of them, and they often used me as an errand boy.

There was such a stark contrast between those smugglers and my father. My dad was just a kind-hearted, simple family man. He was doomed in the ghetto. Day by day, I could see his condition deteriorating. He lost about 60 pounds in a matter of weeks, and although a large portion of my smuggling earnings went towards medicine for him, it was to no avail. A doctor visited frequently and he would tell us he could not prevent the inevitable.

My father died one night in the spring of 1941. He was forty-four. By the time of his death thousands of people had lost their lives in the ghetto, but none had been from my immediate family. I was devastated, having just turned ten.

The next day was a cool, cloudy Friday – another depressing day in the ghetto. They came with a wagon to take my father's body away as though he was a piece of trash. A number of men from our building – including my friend Sevek – acted as pseudo-pall-bearers, carrying his corpse to the wagon.

Once there, he was just piled on. The wagon was filled with bodies, and on its way to collect a few more before going to the Jewish cemetery for yet another day of mass burials. The whole process lacked any shred of decency.

Once my father's body had been collected, the rest of us went to the cemetery. We arrived at about noon, and within a few minutes Menashe spotted my father's remains from among the 50 or so bodies lying on a large table. After waiting around for two long hours until the rabbi arrived, my father and the other dead men and boys were wrapped in a large *talis* (a religious garment) and thrown into a mass grave. The rabbi, an old man with a long white beard, told us to say Kaddish – the Jewish prayer for the dead. Word for word, my brothers and I recited the prayer – hopeful that my father's soul would reach heaven and be embraced by God. My father deserved to go to heaven. He was a sincere, honest, hard-working man. Unfortunately, he was taken away from me in what should have been the prime of his life.

At the funeral, my mother tried hard to hold back her tears. The rest of us cried openly, as any children would at a parent's funeral. However, given the disastrous circumstances of the ghetto, this funeral was much more sombre than those of normal times. It was an extremely difficult experience to deal with. I was traumatized for months. Night after night, I dreamed about all those bodies lying on that table.

The only morsel of satisfaction was that we were able to see my dad laid to rest at least partially in accordance with Jewish tradition. I was also somewhat comforted by the rabbi when he told me it was only my father's body that had died – that his soul was on its way to heaven. And, as I kept telling my mother, at least we had the rest of the family for support.

When the ceremony ended, there was nowhere to go but

home, and there wasn't anything good to go home to. In some ways, my dad was better off. At least his troubles were over; ours were just beginning.

It wasn't long after my father died that my mother began to take a major turn for the worse. Day by day she deteriorated, and it was extremely painful to watch. I had always been very close to my mother, and I have many fond memories of her. Her final days are not among them.

The good days were when I was about seven years old, and I would work with her during my summer holidays. After helping her set up a booth to sell sandals at the farmers' market, it was my job to protect the merchandise so she could concentrate on sales. Professional thieves were all over the place and you had to be vigilant to avoid being targeted. There was no end to the threat. The jails were so overcrowded with convicts that these petty criminals, no matter how many times they were caught, were never kept for long. Usually, they were only sent to jail for a few days and as soon as they were released they were back stealing from people again.

Those days at the market gave me a good chance to watch my mother in action. I had great respect for her talents. Working with her offered a fascinating education in the fundamentals of business, and in particular, how to treat customers properly. I am certain I would not have survived on the streets of Warsaw had it not been for what she taught me.

In fact it was her business acumen that led to one of my most successful smuggling ventures. In late 1941, when the Germans were in desperate need of warm clothes for the Russian front, a decree was issued that forbade Jewish women from possessing any fur. If they owned any, even if it was just a fur collar, they were to hand the pieces over to the Germans during door-to-door collections.

Many Jewish women owned furs and preferred any option over giving theirs to the Germans. People would bury their fur items deep in the ground in boxes, hoping that they would be able to retrieve them when the war ended. Unfortunately, fur dries out and goes rotten when stored this way, leaving the coat worthless – though even the people who knew this felt that burying the garment was much better than giving it away to the Germans.

Late in the summer of 1941, well before the Germans issued their decree but at a time when everyone knew it would happen sooner or later, my mother suggested that I buy furs cheaply from Jews before they had to turn them over. Then, I would sneak out of the Jewish area and sell them to Aryan women for a decent profit.

After succeeding with this and other smuggling schemes, my mother would always say how proud she was of me. She told me that I had a good head for business, and that one day I would grow up to be a successful businessman. That gave me a valuable boost of confidence.

'I will be so proud of you when you grow up and do well for yourself,' she would say. 'Not that I am not proud of you now. I am. I'm proud of all of you. You are wonderful children that any mother would be happy to have. I look forward to the day when you're all grown up and have children of your own.'

It was unbearable to see my mother, once such a vibrant and beautiful woman, in such dire straits. Like my father, she was brokenhearted, feeling totally helpless as she had to watch her children suffer while she couldn't do anything about it. It seemed she just lacked the will to live. She was starving herself to death – insisting that her meagre bread ration go to Eli, as well as her portion of whatever food I smuggled home. As death approached, I suppose the only thing she could look forward to was spending eternity with my father, whom she missed dreadfully.

In the end, her mental and emotional depression led to physical illness in the form of some kind of liver problem, and she went to her grave only a few months after my father's death. Thus I had lost both my parents by September 1941 – more than six months before my eleventh birthday.

What made it most difficult for me was that I was not with my mother when she succumbed. I was out hustling on the Aryan side all day, and when I returned in the evening I heard all kinds of crying as soon as I walked through the door. I knew right away that she had died. I burst out crying. I loved her so much – and still miss her greatly.

Like my father earlier, she had been tossed on to a cart along with several other bodies that had been collected off the streets. This time, however, we never even got to see her remains because she was immediately buried in a mass grave. By then the undertakers were digging countless graves each day, and dumping wagonloads of bodies into them like rubbish. All we could do was say Kaddish with the man responsible for the burials.

My mother was an extraordinarily tough lady, but above all she was a dedicated mother who would – and did – give her life for her children.

With both my parents gone, my sister Brenda took over the reins of the household. She was a lovely young lady of eighteen – about five feet eight inches tall with long dark hair and brown eyes. I remember telling her that if only she had gone to Russia with Getzel maybe she could have had a chance of survival. Maybe she would have even married her boyfriend. She acknowledged that perhaps she should have gone, but it was too late to do anything about it – and besides, at least she was available to help her younger brothers.

'We're all orphans now,' she told us, as tears flowed down all our cheeks. 'The future is so uncertain, but we have to continue to love each other even more. And we have to keep doing our best to survive – day by day. We have to believe that better days will come. In the meantime, I will do my very best to help each of you survive.'

Brenda had always been a big help to me. Not only did she provide me with her dress when I first started smuggling, but soon after that she helped me execute an extremely effective smuggling tactic. In the early ghetto days, there was a streetcar that went through a small portion of the ghetto in order to get from one Aryan street to another quickly. Of course, it never actually stopped in the ghetto – there was no way Jews were going to be allowed on the vehicle. None the less, I found a way to take advantage of the situation.

After crossing to the Aryan side and collecting a bag full of goods, I would go to the end of the line to get on that streetcar. I would stand right next to the conductor – who I had bribed to ignore my smuggling – keeping the bag at my feet. It was shielded from view to all but the conductor. Sometimes there was a Polish policeman on the tram, but he was busy at the back making sure no one jumped on.

Meanwhile, my sister would be waiting at a certain spot in the ghetto, which was alongside the streetcar path. All the conductor had to do was unlock the door next to me as we approached my sister's location. No one would see anything, as I would inconspicuously kick my bag out to her.

Most often, the tram was moving slowly enough that after I kicked the goods out, my sister had enough time to toss me an empty bag with a list telling me what to get next. I made at least four of these trips a day. The conductor took a great risk for us, but I made it worth his while by giving him a large portion of the profit. When I first came up with the idea, I carefully made my sales-pitch to a couple of other streetcar conductors, but could only convince the one to assist me. Fortunately, he was all I needed.

This scheme went on for a month or two, until March 1941 when the Germans changed the streetcar route. But it was wonderful while it lasted, and I remember my mother being particularly proud of our ingenuity.

After we overcame the grief of losing my mother it was back to the regular grind – back to smuggling for survival. As long as our eyes were open our stomachs required food. Unfortunately, not long after returning to my routine, I had a scary incident that put me out of commission for quite a while. I was riding on the tail end of a streetcar one afternoon when I noticed there was a German patrol stopping all the streetcars. I did not know whether they were looking for Jews or a specific individual.

I was about 200 yards from the where the check-point was set up and realized I had to get out of there fast. However, the streetcar was still moving at top speed. None the less, I jumped off and ran for my life. A German saw that I had done this, reached for his rifle, and started to shoot at me.

I ran as fast as I could to the first available opening – a lane between two buildings. A few moments later – still at top speed – I came through to another street that I crossed. Alongside were some railway tracks. As I was running over the tracks my foot got caught and I tumbled down – striking my left knee hard on the metal and slicing it wide open. It began to bleed profusely, but I kept running for a few more minutes and somehow lost the Germans.

I got to a store where I purchased some superficial medication, gauze and rubber bandages. What I really needed was treatment at a hospital – with stitches and real medicine. But I was too scared to go there. I didn't have any identification, and they would ask all kinds of questions about why my parents weren't with me, how it happened and so on. I figured it would be far too risky.

Taking my chances, I laid down for a while and applied pressure to the cut area to stop the bleeding. As soon as I pulled my hand away it started to bleed again. I quickly put a bandage on anyway, and managed to drag myself back through the wall and went straight home to get off my feet.

When I sat down to inspect the knee and change the

bandage, I saw that it was full of pus. It was badly infected, and it hurt like hell. I replaced the bandage with ointment and gauze, then wrapped a couple of bandages around it and hoped for the best. For the next few days, I had a difficult time, and stayed off my left leg as much as possible. In fact, it took almost a year to heal completely. To this day, there is a very distinctive red scar on my knee as a reminder of that incident.

That recovery probably wouldn't have taken as long if I hadn't done so much damage to my knees in the previous year of smuggling. Many times I had to scale the ghetto wall and jump to the ground. Often I was weighed down with goods. This took its toll on my knees, and at one stage a doctor told me I had retained a lot of water in my knees and if I didn't rest for a while I would do serious damage. Of course I never took his advice or we would have starved to death.

This time, however, I couldn't operate as if my health was perfect: I had to turn to less physical tactics, so I began begging. It was less lucrative, but much better than doing nothing. I put my cross around my neck and started to sing in front of apartment buildings where the richer people lived. Sometimes I sang religious songs so no one would suspect that I was not a Christian. And I always made sure my hair was cut very short and straight because I had a naturally curly head of hair which was rare for gentiles. I was also confident no one would suspect my Jewish identity because there were many Polish women and children who were so poor they too were begging.

Whenever I sang people would throw down some bread or a few pennies. Occasionally, someone would even call me up and give me a plate of home-cooked food. What a treat that was. Usually, however, I returned home with a very hoarse voice, a little cash and a bag filled with bread, potatoes and cabbage. Each evening Brenda would make soup and we had a very hearty meal considering the conditions that surrounded us.

While I managed to handle the day-to-day life of crossing the wall, Menashe had a much more difficult time. I must admit, however, that it was courageous of him to try to shoulder the smuggling burden alone while I recovered from my knee injury. It was too bad that he wasn't well-suited for the work, as he had more than his share of troubles.

One of his scariest moments came one afternoon as he was approaching the wall with a large bag of potatoes on his back. Some gentile children were hanging around the ghetto wall on the Aryan side. These individuals, known as 'shmaltzers', used to know what the Jewish kids were doing, and would try to steal from us as we came close to the wall. You had to be both careful and lucky to avoid them, though it was better to be confronted by a few schmaltzers than to have to face a German guard.

When several of these hoodlums demanded money from Menashe he told them he didn't have any. One of the boys then pulled out a knife. He lunged forward, jabbing the knife toward the sack Menashe was carrying. The boy was trying to rip open the bag so all the potatoes would fall out. Sensing the attack, Menashe quickly turned around and took the swipe of the blade with his hand. Bleeding profusely, somehow he ran away from them and made it back through the wall – without even losing any potatoes. We took him to a Jewish doctor, who stitched up the wounds for the payment of two potatoes.

Shortly after that incident, however, Menashe came home with a high fever and stomach pains. He had contracted typhus, which was rampant in the ghetto in the fall of 1941. With that and his injured hand, it was the end of his smuggling for a while. Then things went from bad to worse about a week later when I too came down with the disease.

Having typhus is not a pleasant experience. Your temperature shoots way up, you have chills, severe weakness, pains in all your limbs and suffer from severe headaches. Hallucinations are also typical. As well, on about the fourth or fifth day a rash appears on your skin, which spreads throughout your body.

Typhus was a disease that proved to be deadly for thousands of Jews in the ghetto. There was no way you could get any medicine for it because a single tube of anti-typhus serum cost several thousand zlotys. You just had to hope for the best from your immune system.

Now that Menashe and I were both flat on our backs we had a problem. Even if we survived, how were we all going to eat? Fortunately, I had planned ahead in case something like this would happen. Some of my smuggling days were extremely profitable. On those occasions I would put away some of the money as insurance. Without telling anyone, I had hidden the cash in the cuffs of my pants.

While we were ill, I told my sister not to worry too much because I had saved some money. At first she didn't believe me. She thought I was babbling nonsense as a result of my fever. I had to convince her to hand me my pants to prove it. I reached in and pulled out 500 zlotys. It wasn't a fortune, but it was enough to keep us going until I recovered. She literally jumped for joy at the sight. She wanted to kiss me, but realized that wasn't a good idea if she wanted to avoid being infected with the disease.

Menashe and I both recovered, although we were severely weakened for quite some time by two precarious weeks on what at times felt like our deathbeds. We were also lucky that Brenda and my little brother Eli didn't catch the disease.

After a couple of weeks, we ran out of money. I was not fully recovered – either from the typhus or my knee – but we desperately needed income again. I felt I was strong enough to get back to my regular routine of crossing over to the Aryan side of the ghetto. Menashe did the same, while Brenda stayed home with Eli.

Life proceeded 'normally' into the first few months of 1942, but in the early spring our next crisis struck. Brenda became seriously ill with some kind of infection and was rushed to the ghetto's hospital. Unfortunately, it wasn't a typical hospital. There was neither medicine nor food. It was up to the relatives to come and feed the patients. So when I came to visit her each afternoon, I would bring buttered bread and the occasional apple or pear.

With the burden already becoming heavier, we were dealt another blow shortly after Brenda entered the hospital. Menashe had been caught trying to smuggle food back into the ghetto, and was put in the jail at 24 Gesia. The site, which consisted of a number of adjoined structures, had previously served as a Polish military prison. In May 1942 there were about 1,300 Jews detained in the jail. All of the inmates suffered from starvation and were close to collapse. About 200 of them, including my brother, were children who had been caught smuggling, and they were kept in a separate section.

When I used to say that I was eight years old in order to receive lenient treatment from the authorities, I could get away with it because I looked so young. Menashe couldn't. He was a tall 13-year-old who looked older than his age. Though he was lucky to not be killed, he was held indefinitely, which was, in effect, a death sentence anyway because they gave the inmates virtually no food. The only way to help him survive was to bribe the guard to take some food to him. That put an extra strain on me. I now had two siblings to deliver food to – one in hospital and one in jail.

I didn't want to tell Brenda that Menashe was caught. I was afraid it would upset her and she would become sicker. I told her he had a bad cold, and didn't want to visit for fear of worsening her illness. I delayed telling the truth as long as I could – until I was sure she was strong enough to handle the bad news.

At home I was alone with my younger brother Eli and it was

extremely difficult for both of us. I was constantly on the go – begging on the Aryan side, and running back and forth between the jail and the hospital. Sensing the gravity of the situation, precocious Eli insisted on helping me. He figured we could double our income, and I decided we had little choice but to give it a try.

We continued with the singing and begging tactics I had recently initiated, and spent most of our time doing it together. Sometimes we'd jump on streetcars as they were loading up at the main terminal. We'd beg from person to person, and some of them would toss spare change into our hats. Other times, we sang Polish songs on street corners. The people who walked by would give us some spare change, and over time we would accumulate enough zlotys to buy a decent amount of food. We would smuggle that back into the ghetto and distribute it to both Brenda and Menashe. This had to be done each and every day.

I remember one of those mornings heading off to the Aryan side when little Eli received quite a scare. As he was squeezing his way through a hole in the wall, a Polish policeman was standing off to the side waiting for him. Eli poked his arms and head out of the hole and was scanning for guards when the policeman suddenly grabbed him and repeatedly struck his head and hands with a stick. Eli screamed and cried and frantically yelled for me to pull him back in. I managed to, but he didn't come away unscathed. His blue eyes were all black, his head was all swelled up and sore, and he couldn't move his hands properly for weeks. Had it gone on much longer, I think he would have been beaten to death. The incident greatly frightened Eli but he was remarkably tough, and didn't let it deter him from smuggling. From then on, however, he would only climb the wall, never trusting the holes. He was quite an agile little guy because it was a 10-foot climb up the wall, and there was no climbing down the other side – he had to jump.

Our struggle went on for a few more weeks until one day we received the excellent news that Brenda was to be released. When she left the hospital I told her about Menashe. She was very shocked and upset, but she also realized there was nothing she could do, and her immediate task was to take care of Eli and me. Even during such difficult times she maintained a sense of optimism as she assumed the role of mother and father. However, circumstances were still to get much worse, and it wouldn't be long until optimism became all but impossible.

4 • The Final Solution

Despite everything the Germans had done so far, their desire systematically to murder us in gas chambers was beyond our imagination. We had hoped their battles with the Russians would eventually lead to the realization that Jews could be an exploitable resource for the war effort. So in the spring of 1942, when rumours started to circulate that they were going to take everyone out of the ghetto, we figured they wanted to put us to work in places such as armament factories.

One afternoon, there was talk on the street that early the next day the Germans were going to enter the ghetto to collect people. Sensing that the Germans wanted slave labour, my sister felt it was best for Eli and me to leave the ghetto that night and stay permanently on the Aryan side. She said that if there was a door-to-door round-up, she had a better chance of surviving because she was a young, energetic woman who could be used for labour, while we were just little kids who were expendable. She also reminded us that neither of us had Jewish appearances, and that we were streetwise enough to survive on the outside.

I didn't like the idea of separating, and told her we would only go if she came with us. 'You go first,' she responded. 'You can get established over there and then I'll follow. You can adapt better there. As little kids, you can sleep anywhere and can always beg for food.' She insisted that we listen to her because she was the oldest remaining child, and was doing what my parents would have wanted.

As a compromise, I said I would go if she allowed me to return to check on her every couple of days – and to bring food and money to her. She agreed to that, and the discussion was over. The rest of the day we quietly got ourselves organized to leave that night.

Just before we left, the silence was broken when Brenda couldn't hold back the tears any longer. 'What have they done to our family?' she asked rhetorically. Eli and I started to cry as well, and we embraced her, trying to console each other by saying that everything would turn out OK eventually. I promised her that I would take good care of Eli.

In choosing where to leave the ghetto, we had to be extremely cautious because the guards worked rotating eight-hour shifts to ensure 24-hour surveillance. I picked the part of the wall that was adjacent to the market, believing the stalls in the area would provide a number of hiding places that were only a short distance from the ghetto.

After getting to the top of the wall, we looked around carefully and didn't see any German soldiers or Polish police. We jumped down to the other side, and scrambled into the market area. We hid among the stands and prayed for the best. After our hearts slowed down and we felt comfortable that no one was around, we drifted off to sleep for the night. We couldn't go anywhere because any Pole caught outdoors after the 9 p.m. curfew could be shot.

Unfortunately, we slept for a little longer than we would have liked, and were still asleep at dawn when the curfew ended. We were awakened by the woman who owned the stall we were in. 'Jesus Christ, you nearly gave me a heart attack,' she yelled out. 'Who the hell are you? What are you doing here?'

Startled and acting on instinct, we yelled back – telling her that we were poor kids who had run away from home because our father beat us up. We said we needed a place to sleep and her booth was the right place at the right time.

As we got to our feet we calmed down. We thanked her and apologized for the inconvenience. That seemed to soften her demeanour, and as we prepared to leave she gave each of us a piece of fresh bread. We were starving so we really appreciated the gesture.

Pleased that we were now off to a good start, we hopped on to a streetcar that took us over to Grochowska Street – a place where we had a lot of success begging and singing. More importantly, it was where Mr and Mrs Slawcia had their little café.

I explained our predicament to them and asked if my little brother and I could stay in their restaurant until the tension in the ghetto subsided. Fortunately, they agreed to take us in. That meant a lot to me. They knew we were Jewish, so they could suffer the death penalty if caught – but they helped us anyway. I trusted them completely, and it gave me peace of mind to know we were safe there at night.

To minimize the risk to the Slawcias, we would stay on the streets until just before curfew. We also needed the full day to come up with food required for our siblings' survival. Sometimes Eli and I would work together; other times we would split up and I would go back to the ghetto. I always went back alone because I felt that if there was a German attack while I was in the ghetto at least Eli would survive by remaining on the Aryan side.

The Germans didn't liquidate the ghetto as the rumours had suggested, nor did they over the next few days, so I was free to go back and deliver food to Menashe, and then to Brenda. I also made some extra money by carrying messages from adult smugglers on the Aryan side to their colleagues in the ghetto. What's more, I took some additional groceries with me, which I exchanged for clothing, and after selling those items back on the Aryan side I was able to make even more money.

When I met up with Brenda we hugged with joy and relief to see each other again. 'How is Eli?' she asked. 'I miss him so much. How I long to hold him close to me.' I told her how I kept close watch on him as he spent his day singing songs at the streetcar stand across the street from where I would kneel down and beg. He was well-suited for the work – even more Aryan-looking than me with blond hair and a small snub nose. He also spoke excellent Polish, and could handle the physical rigours, as he was larger and taller than me, despite our age difference.

I told Brenda that he had quickly become accustomed to life on the Aryan side, and was earning more than his share on the streets. At the end of the day we used to compare who had made more money and he beat me every day. And that didn't take into account the occasional sandwich he used to be given – something that happened to me much less frequently.

Brenda smiled as she listened to the update, and asked if there was a way I could bring Eli with me for a visit. I said I would do my best.

Three days later the Germans still hadn't done anything, so I brought Eli with me into the ghetto. He too had been asking me each day when he'd be able to see his sister again, so when the opportunity came he was quite excited. It was a heartening visit – a few moments of happiness before our world was turned upside down yet again.

All of the rumours that had been circulating eventually came true. On 19 July 1942 – unknown to us at the time – the Germans had ordered the ghetto be wiped out by the end of the year, and the process was to begin just a few days later. Starting on 22 July, thousands of Jews per day were to be taken away to the gas chambers of Treblinka – which commenced operations on 23 July.

I was in the ghetto on the morning of 22 July – visiting some smuggling friends after seeing my sister. When my friends noticed that troops were gathering around the ghetto, they suggested it would be best that I remain with them.

By 9 a.m., Lithuanian, Latvian, Ukrainian and German

soldiers had surrounded the ghetto, while several trucks had entered in order to collect Jews. The *Judenrat* (the Jewish administration of the ghetto) and their Jewish 'police' were to carry out the dirty work under the watchful eyes of the foreign troops.

There were blockades of many houses in the area. All entrances and exits to the dwellings were closed. All tenants were then ordered to come out, present their documents, and be prepared to leave. The Jewish police inspected the apartments to make sure all the inhabitants had complied with the order. We could discern no pattern as to which houses were being selected.

Most people who were caught thought they were just being sent to a labour camp, so they voluntarily marched off. They were told the round-ups were for a 'resettlement in the East'. Each deportee was permitted to take along some luggage and all their valuables.

They were taken to the Umshlagplatz – a large yard that merged into the railway tracks, and which bordered on to the back of the hospital Brenda had stayed in. The hospital had been evacuated earlier in July, and was converted into an overly cramped, filthy holding area for the train platform.

The unlucky souls to be 'resettled' were moved from the hospital to the Umshlagplatz and then into enclosed cattle trains. They crammed some 100–120 men, women and children into those railcars. Without food, water or ventilation the conditions were sub-standard even for cattle. As a result, the many who were weak died in transit.

Those who survived the trip were told upon arrival that they were to take a shower and would then be fed. They were stripped and taken into large rooms where showerheads were hooked up to the ceiling. Instead of water, however, zyclon gas came through the showerheads. It only took a few minutes to kill cleanly scores of people – a stroke of disgustingly efficient, sadistic genius. The bodies were then inspected, and gold tooth-fillings were extracted and set aside. The flesh and bones were then turned to ashes in crematorium ovens. The camps were nothing more than death factories.

My adult friends – who were about to transform from smugglers to freedom-fighters – were not naïve. They didn't believe a word of the German propaganda. They insisted that we keep a low profile until the Germans relented. Fortunately, the Germans stayed away from the houses on our street. None the less, we didn't take any chances. The smuggling leaders were the only ones who ventured outside – occasionally getting us food and water.

With such tight security around the walls – and the risk of being taken away if I wandered on to the wrong street at the wrong time – I realized there was no option but to stay put and let the adults take the risks. I could only hope that my sister was staying hidden too. I felt reasonably assured that Eli was safe on the outside, but I was worried sick about Menashe. Jail was not the place to be under such circumstances.

With nowhere to go, I spent a lot of time getting close to the dozen or so people in our flat. There was a couple there I particularly liked named Joe and Chawa. They had a two-year-old daughter named Schajadala. Knowing how bad things were, and to give the child a chance to survive, the couple had recently given her away to a gentile family who lived on a farm. The farmers were well paid to take care of Schajadala, and the deal was that if either birth parent survived the war, they would be able to get the child back.

Chawa was a nervous wreck; she had tears in her eyes all day long. Joe kept his emotions more to himself, but it was obvious by the pain on his face that he was devastated too. They were full of guilt over what they had done, but were only thinking of the child's welfare and just wanted her to have the chance to grow up and have a decent life. I think they made the right decision; survival in the ghetto in the summer of 1942 seemed impossible.

By the last few days of July, while I remained in hiding with Joe, Chawa and the others, people in the ghetto began to figure out what the Germans were up to, and stopped handing themselves over voluntarily. More and more stories filtered back about what was happening at the camps. Those few who managed to escape told us that people there had virtually no chance of survival. I recall being told a story by one of our leaders about a father who was given labour duty to stave off death for a few days. His job was to shove dead bodies into the ovens, including his own family.

With less cooperation from their victims, the Germans, Ukrainians, Lithuanians and Latvians became more active – doing more of the work themselves and more forcefully directing the Jewish police. Deportations consequently became increasingly haphazard and unpredictable. People were dragged away from their homes without their bags. To try to get more volunteers to come to the Umshlagplatz, they enticed people with bread and marmalade. Some people were so hungry they went for it – even if they realized it meant probable death.

The soldiers also began grabbing more people randomly off the streets – and they initiated extremely aggressive housing raids. That was when things got difficult for us. One morning, after I had been in our flat for nearly a week, we were woken up by a warning. 'Get up, get up,' we were told in a panic. 'The Germans have entered the ghetto in massive numbers! They're going to raid all the buildings.'

We got dressed very quickly, and via a network of connections from rooftop to rooftop, we rushed to a hiding place at 17 Wolynska – ironically located across the street from where I was born. It was a much larger, better-hidden place than the flat we had been staying in.

There were about 70 men, women and children in that attic. Everyone was scared, but for the most part managed to remain calm. Late in the morning, we heard the Germans roam around the staircase beneath us, but somehow they never found us. We had survived for the moment.

We were among the fortunate. With the help of the traitorous ghetto police, the soldiers hauled off many more Jews than on any of the previous days. All I could think about was my sister. Where was she hiding during these apartment raids? I wanted to leave the safe haven and rush over to her place, but Joe held me back. He said I would likely get caught by the Germans and that would be the end of me.

'But what about my sister?' I kept repeating. 'She is all alone right now worrying about me. I'm safe here, but I have no idea what's happened to her.'

Still, he was wisely persistent in not letting me go. 'She is probably in some bunker hiding too,' he said. 'You'd never find her.'

I respected and admired Joe so much I felt compelled to listen to him. During the discussion, he said to me: 'You will survive if you are destined to. It's the same for your sister. Just hang in there as best you can, and let destiny take its course.'

He was so stoic about everything. In our new hiding place, we talked more about his daughter, and he said he had accepted the reality that he would never have the joy of seeing her grow up. He knew he wasn't going to survive the war, and he insisted he wasn't going to die quietly when his time came. I found such talk very inspirational.

By nightfall, after the Germans had gathered their sizable capture of Jews for the day, the liquidation was temporarily suspended from our area. With the scene quieted down, some of the men left the hiding place in search of food and to find out what happened to some of their friends. I went with them, and while I had the opportunity, dashed over to my sister's place to see if she was OK.

There were a few people milling about in front of her building. They were from the building next door and had managed to get by undetected. They told me that Brenda's building had been raided, and that she was taken away along with about 20 others.

I felt my heart sink to the ground with crushing sadness. And before I had time fully to absorb the blow, there was more bad news. The Gesia prison housing Menashe was close by, so I asked the group if they knew what the situation was there. They said the prison had been emptied a few days ago, and that all the boys and girls had been shipped off. The Germans' barbarism was incomprehensible – all the beautiful little children had been exterminated as if they were animals. Menashe was one of these guinea pigs – gassed at Treblinka to determine how 'well' the system worked before the mass killings took place.

Menashe and Brenda were now gone. I cried and cried, oblivious to the people around me. I vomited what little food was in my gut and ran back to our hiding place.

In the midst of my crying, I told the tragedy that besieged me to everyone else in the attic. While I knew in my heart that things had really hit rock bottom, they tried to comfort me and told me not to give up hope. By that point I was numb – I knew I'd never see my lovely sister and dear brother again. There are no words to describe the pain I felt that night.

I managed to keep from breaking down completely only because there wasn't much time to think. I just wanted to get the hell out of the ghetto and be with my one remaining sibling – my brother Eli who was still on the Aryan side. I also didn't feel safe in the ghetto. Just because the Germans didn't discover us this time, it didn't mean we would be so lucky again tomorrow. The next morning I decided to move.

The only people the Germans did not round up were a few Jewish labourers with special passes. The Nazis had figured it was best to get what they could out of the healthiest Jews before killing them. Each day the workers would leave for their slave duty on the outside. I decided they would be my vehicle out of the ghetto. A friend in the hideout told me where a group of them would gather each morning.

I went to that location, where I saw a group of about 100–200 young and strong Jewish men beginning to congregate. As the men waited for the Germans to arrive, I talked to a couple who confirmed that they were going to work on the Aryan side. I asked if I could join them as a way to get out of the ghetto. I was told that I was too small and if the Germans spotted me they would immediately shoot me. They said I was crazy. But they didn't say no. Having just lost my brother and sister, I didn't care. I was either going to see my little brother or die.

As I marched with the men I somehow remained quite inconspicuous. I was so small I was tough to spot among all the big bodies. And I was lucky that these Jews helped me – doing their best to shield me from the Germans' view. I took off as soon as we crossed the gate to the Aryan side, running as fast as I could. I still don't know how I made it – total luck I suppose that there were only a couple of Germans guarding that whole group of men.

I jumped on the tail of a streetcar going to Praga, and went down to Grochowska Street where my little brother was staying. As soon as I came in the door, I leapt into his arms. I was so happy to see that he was fine, and he was relieved to see that I was alive.

Eli and I clung to one another – knowing that all we had now was each other. The Slawcias were also happy to see me. They said they thought they'd never see me alive again. In a brief moment of morbid levity, I told them I was a cat with nine lives, and that I still had a couple more to use up.

Once the warmth of our exchange wore off, I told Eli about Brenda and Menashe. It took a moment or two until the reality hit him. We cried our eyes out, and it wasn't until several minutes later that he spoke: 'If it's just you and me who are left out of our entire family which one of us is next?'

I assured him that I would look out for him and that we would both make it. We would survive the war, I said, and have some great times together in the years to come. We hugged again with tears in our eyes.

A few days later, as we were feeling extremely depressed still grieving over our loss, we somehow had a particularly good day on the streets. That evening, I said we should get something good to eat, as a way to lift our spirits. My brother suggested having a small glass of whiskey. It seemed he had been exposed to the café's famous drink while I had been away. He really did have a mischievous side to him. I had already caught him smoking a cigarette once. In fact, he had a pack and some matches in his pocket. I gave him hell for it.

This time the drinking led to a new lecture from me. 'You're only ten years old,' I said. 'Why are you going to drink booze at such a young age? A glass of milk would be more appropriate.'

He said that one time when I was away, Mrs Slawcia had given him a shot of the whiskey with some pepper in it to calm his upset stomach. I told him that didn't make it right – and that he'd better promise never to smoke or drink – 'or else'.

'Or else what?' he asked.

'Or else I'll have nothing to do with you anymore,' I replied.

'You must be kidding,' he said. 'You smoke. And I've seen you drink.'

'You are only ten years old. I am twelve. When you get to be my age, I'll let you smoke and drink too,' I said facetiously as we both smiled. Then a look of concern came over his face.

'What if I don't make it to twelve?' he asked.

'Don't talk like that,' I snapped back. 'You must have a more positive attitude. We will both survive the war and have great lives when this is all over. You'll see.' He smiled again and hugged me. He also promised not to smoke or drink. And to the best of my knowledge, he kept that promise.

As the liquidation continued in the ghetto, I survived on the Aryan streets with Eli. I became emotionally confused as I followed from afar the atrocities taking place in the ghetto. I didn't know what to think anymore. On the one hand, now that I knew the Germans' 'master plan' to exterminate the Jews, I promised myself that I would never be taken alive; I vowed never to allow them to ship me to the gas chambers. Dying was acceptable, provided I died with a purpose. I just wanted revenge – a chance to be able to fight back in some way.

I could not comprehend why for so long we hadn't organized ourselves and obtained some weapons to fight for our murdered parents, brothers and sisters. We already had one cheek slapped and now we were turning our face so the other side could be smacked as well. If I only I was an adult, I thought, I could organize some resistance. I visualized myself dying heroically in battle.

On the other hand – and the part of me that eventually prevailed – I really wanted to live, to see the Nazi regime pay for what it had done. More importantly, I kept telling Eli that we would survive – that one day we would get married and be the seeds replenishing the Klajman family. 'The tree will grow like wildfire,' I would tell him.

That is not to say that we weren't realistic. We figured there was maybe a one-in-a-hundred chance of survival, but that was good enough for hope. As my grown-up smuggler-friend Joe told me: 'Where there is hope there is life, and where there is life there is hope.' I thought it was a great phrase, and I kept repeating it to Eli. 'Have hope, we must have hope. Every day of survival is one more day of hope.' Eli and I were a great team – two brothers who loved one another, and got along like best friends.

Often, on days when we didn't do too well begging, we had no choice but to steal food in order to survive. I remember stealing from the twice-weekly farmers' market in the summer and early fall. I took turnips, apples, carrots – whatever was easiest at that moment. I remember several autumn breakfasts of cold turnip.

Eli, on the other hand, was much better at the game than me. He never chose the easiest picking. He went for what he wanted most – and that wasn't turnip. He wanted to steal fresh bread and baked goods.

I could never figure out how he did it. No matter how carefully the food was guarded, he always seemed to get his hands on what he was after. And it wasn't often that he was caught. Only occasionally would he get over-anxious and make himself conspicuous when he grabbed the item. And even then, he was always quick enough to get away.

One time he was caught stealing a loaf of bread. As he scrambled off, the merchant ran up to him and gave him a hard kick in the butt. As soon as Eli met up with me an hour later, the first thing he did was kick me in the behind.

'You said we should share everything 50/50. Well that's your half,' he said. We both laughed as we enjoyed the bread.

Between the two of us, we were making enough to eat every day. The only problem was where to sleep at night. Things had been fine until a grease fire in August destroyed Mr and Mrs Slawcia's café. They weren't harmed but they lost everything they owned and had to move to the countryside and stay with relatives.

The one fortunate aspect to the fire was that it occurred in summertime, when shelter wasn't as vital as in winter. On clear nights, we could sleep in the cornfields, or in the park among the large, dense trees. One priority we had was to stay clean, and that was one advantage to the park; it bordered on the Vistula so we could wash ourselves and our clothes in the river. We cleaned ourselves for health reasons and for security. If we were too dirty, we could give ourselves away.

On rainy nights we had to look for shelter, which could be a problem. The first couple of wet nights were very scary. We managed to find a couple of apartment attics, but that was risky. You could easily be caught and turned over, and it was unwise to stay in the same place twice because that could arouse suspicion.

Then one afternoon we stumbled across an idea which solved our problem. I saw a large piece of land where vegetables were growing. After we stole a few tomatoes, a man who spotted our theft started chasing us. We got away easily, and he was unable recognize us so it was a harmless event.

We noticed that the man had come out of a shed that was adjacent to the field. He was a nightwatchman paid to make sure people like us or more important criminals didn't steal any produce. The shed looked as if it would offer protection – that man was the only person in sight for quite a distance.

It was obvious that he wasn't making much money in his job – working seven nights a week for a rich tomato-grower. So I offered him rent if he'd let us stay in the shed on rainy nights. He was all for the idea – it was extra money and he didn't have to do anything. Plus he felt good about doing it – helping two boys he thought were Christian orphans.

We told him that our father was an alcoholic who beat us every day, and that he also beat our mother who fled one day with another man because she could no longer tolerate the abuse. We said we didn't like the boyfriend, and made her choose between him and us. She chose him. We explained that we had no option but to run away, and it was up to me to take care of little 'Wiesrek' – our Polish name for Eli, just as my Polish alias was Janek. After we told the watchman our story he took great pity on us. He would often give us soup and sometimes even let us stay for free.

Back in the ghetto, the Germans finally stopped their daily collection of Jews in mid-September. By that point, some 300,000 people – the vast majority of the total ghetto population – had been sent to their extermination.

I had been on the outside for nearly two months so I was full of curiosity about the ghetto and felt compelled to return. I still had lots of unanswered questions, including what had happened to the people I was with – particularly my friend Joe, who had so graciously taken me under his wing in that hiding spot. I was also anxious to make some money. Ghetto smuggling paid far more handsomely than begging, and now that things had returned to 'normal' in the ghetto it seemed the ideal time to return.

Having spent several weeks with Eli, I was pleased that he was doing so well under such difficult circumstances. I felt he was tough enough to be left on his own while I went back to the ghetto. When I said I was going to take a day or two away from him, his first reaction was fear. He was worried that I would never come back and he'd be left abandoned.

I explained that I would be back, and that it really was necessary that I go – not just to check up on my friends, but as a way to make some much-needed money. He didn't like the idea, but he understood my reasons, and told me to hurry back as soon as I could.

That autumn day, I slipped back into the ghetto through a hole in the wall. I remember it was a Friday, and I had brought some fish with me to sell for the Sabbath dinner. By this point, there weren't that many people left in the ghetto, and even fewer who could afford to pay for the food. But I found them. I exchanged the food for clothing – the only article of value left. I felt sorry for these people, but at least they were lucky enough to be able to eat when so many others had died.

Once I finished with that business, I used the rest of my time in the ghetto to determine what happened to those who were in the bunker with me at the beginning of the Aktion (the operation involving the mass assembly, deportation, and murder of Jews by the Nazis during the Holocaust) – especially Joe. I met up with a few surviving smuggling friends in the Jewish underground – a rendezvous I had pre-arranged through a contact on the Aryan side. These men had been friends with Joe.

They told me that Joe was rounded up to go to Treblinka just like all the others. Other than me, the smuggling leaders who had been out getting food at the time of the raid were the only survivors from the group.

Joe had said he would do something special when captured, and he kept his word. Just before turning himself in to be taken away, he hid a large pair of pincers in his shirt. I suspect he may have thought he'd be able to cut through the fence of the camp to escape, or maybe he just wanted a weapon.

Whatever his motive, when Joe got to the Umshlagplatz, he had apparently been verbally abused by a German officer. Joe reacted by pulling out the pincers and jumping on the officer – cutting his throat and digging in – refusing to let go.

Joe was about 35 years of age and one of the biggest and strongest men I knew. He kept digging deeper and deeper into the Nazi's throat, even as several Germans pumped round after round of ammunition into his possessed body. He died still firmly gripping the pliers, which had long ago killed the Gestapo man. He had ripped his throat to pieces.

To me, he was the greatest hero in the world. People talked about his courage for months after that incident. Although he fell to the ground as another dead Jew, at least he had taken a

German with him. He was a valiant martyr. Perhaps more than any other individual in the war, he was the most inspirational to me. I am proud to have known him, and proud to have considered him my friend and idol.

As for his wife, I believe she was loaded on to a train, and met her end at Treblinka. I do not know what ever became of their daughter. I assume she married a Pole and lived the life of a gentile – never knowing her true heritage. It's too bad because I remember asking Joe and Chawa to tell me where Schajadala was. I thought that if I survived the war and they didn't I could find their daughter and pass on the truth of her past. But they refused to give me the information, fearing that if I was captured and tortured I might reveal the story.

My trip to the ghetto brought me nothing but sad news. The vast majority of my smuggling friends who were my age had been taken away to Treblinka. All the older friends I had made in the bunker were gone too. I felt overcome with bitter hatred. I hated the Germans, I hated the Poles and I hated the Jews who collaborated with the Nazis when they came in to round us up.

I couldn't understand how a civilized nation like Germany could do such unspeakable things. And what of the Poles? There were some brave ones who helped us, but many were indifferent to our plight and sometimes just as bad or even worse than the Germans. Worst of all, I couldn't believe there actually were Jews who thought they might survive by turning in other Jews. Those that helped the Germans were given better rations, but ultimately they too were shipped out to concentration camps and were gassed alongside those they had betrayed.

I just wanted to get out of there, and return to my brother. I slipped through the wall and made it back to Grochowska Street before curfew. When I greeted Eli, he was just as excited and relieved to see me as the night the Aktion began.

'Eli, don't worry about me,' I joked with him. 'I'm indestructible. I'm on a mission to get both of us to survive this rotten war.'

As September gave way to October, our farm-shed haven was locked up for the season. It was back to the daily search for shelter during fall and winter. We made hiding places out of basements, attics and whatever other nooks and crannies were available in apartment buildings. We would take straw mats that people left out in front of their apartment doors and use them as mattresses. An empty potato bag was our blanket. We both climbed inside and slept close to one another to gain the benefit of maximum body heat.

Our nomadic existence was both risky and stressful. Following the Aktion, the Germans were aware that some Jews had escaped the ghetto and were living clandestinely on the Aryan side. To weed us out, they used a carrot-and-stick approach with the Poles. The death penalty had been decreed for any Pole found helping hide a Jew, but they also offered three kilos of sugar to any Pole who turned a Jew over to the authorities. There were billboards everywhere promoting it. Unfortunately, many Poles seized the opportunity.

That is why we slept in different places every night. Even when begging and singing we didn't stay in one place for too long. It didn't matter if we were really successful there; we had to move around a lot so no one got too suspicious.

One day towards the end of 1942 Eli and I had just chosen a particular apartment block to sing in when two children approached us. Normally, we kept our distance from everyone to keep our identities secret, but occasionally we would chat – just so we didn't look too paranoid.

We conducted nothing more than small talk for a few minutes with these two boys, but somehow they must have figured out that we were Jews. Perhaps it was because they sensed we were in a similar predicament. In fact, in a rare and dangerous display of candour, they stunned us by saying they were Jews. Once the shock wore off we couldn't help but smile. It was great to know that someone else was going through the same experience as we were. The boys' names were Zenek and Pavel. They were brothers who had been rounded up during the first liquidation attempt, but had managed to get out of their train car on the way to Treblinka. They had some tools with them which enabled them to prise open the door.

They both jumped out of that moving train and luckily were unhurt. They got back to Warsaw, but stayed out of the ghetto. They were like us in that they spoke good Polish and could pass as Christian boys.

There was also another boy we met in a similar manner. His name was Zybyszek. He was a very independent-minded, strong character who was a year or two older than me. He was particularly Aryan-looking, and used this to great advantage as he found work with a merchant in the market. As time went on, he became my closest friend, and our group of five often hung out together.

In early winter, when the choice of attics and basements became even more limited, Eli and I finally found somewhere to stay. It was an old horse stable in an area which had been re-zoned for apartment buildings. We lived in a unit that still had hay on the ground. We had to pay rent – which wasn't too expensive considering it was a horse stable.

Unlike the Slawcias, we never trusted the elderly couple who were our landlords. We didn't dare say that we were Jewish. And they never asked – knowing that ignorance was bliss if trouble ever arose. But it must have crossed their minds. After all, why else would two children be sleeping in horse hay?

Now that there was a safe place for Eli, I decided to get back to smuggling full-time. He could beg on the Aryan side while I made larger sums with my adult friends. I needed extra money to be able to pay the rent, plus the additional income would allow us to eat a lot better – and with the cold winter upon us it became even more important to be decently nourished.

Each trip back to the ghetto reinforced my bitterness. Faced with such a hostile environment that was only getting worse, why can't the Jews in the ghetto fight back, I kept asking myself. Why did we have to be cowards, acting like sheep being sent to the slaughter? There had to be a way to put up some resistance.

The battle finally came – the only problem was that it was too little, too late.

5 • The Uprising

If God or no one else on the planet was going to stop the Germans, it was up to us to defend ourselves.

The last time I remembered Jews fighting in any meaningful way was before the war. Groups of hooligans were often on the hunt for Jews, terrorizing us whenever the opportunity presented itself. Skirmishes were common, and the usual result was that most of the outnumbered Jews were stabbed to death or at least seriously injured.

One time, however, several of the tougher Jewish boys in my neighbourhood sought retribution. Armed with knives and steel chains, they rented a horse-and-buggy and went over to the Aryan gangs' neighbourhoods. Using what could be called 'commando' tactics, they gave the thugs a taste of their own medicine – teaching them that attacking us could result in painful consequences. If only we had embraced this attitude on a mass scale early in the war, we could have dramatically altered the course of events.

The Aktion of mid-1942 had completely changed the face of the ghetto. By the end of the year there were only 40,000 Jews remaining, spread out among three zones which were separated by large stretches of evacuated territory. There was the 'Brushmakers' Shop' area, which contained a brush factory and other little shops, the 'Little Toebbens' Area' – another enterprise zone – and the central ghetto. Jews were officially not allowed to move from one zone to another, but in practice this was not strictly enforced so people moved around quite freely.

The temporary calm the Germans had created could not deceive us. Perhaps the devastation of the Aktion was the final straw, but people in the ghetto finally realized death was certain to come sooner or later, and that there was nothing to lose by resisting.

With no fear of death, we were energized to fight to the best of our abilities. Everyone knew the chance of victory was zero, but winning wasn't the goal. We just wanted to die with dignity. This attitude gave me a sense of pride and satisfaction. It was wonderful to see everyone pull together with such great purpose. I knew that if any Jews in the country would stand up and fight, it would be the Warsaw Ghetto Jews.

For us to have any success we had to obtain weapons. Much of our arsenal was home-made – most notably Molotov cocktails. The rest had to be purchased, which was difficult though not impossible. Opportunities began to emerge as more and more Germans and their allies passed through Warsaw upon their return from the Eastern Front. After major losses against the Russians, many of these soldiers were desperate for cash. Some were willing to sell their weapons, and this accounted for a significant portion of the Jewish arsenal. Other guns were obtained from Poles who had hidden their weapons when the Germans took control of Poland in 1939. As well, a few Poles who worked in armament factories in and around Warsaw managed to smuggle out some items which they would sell to our fighters.

One of our biggest challenges was paying for the goods. Millions of zlotys were needed. Guns cost 12,000 zlotys apiece, the price of a bullet was 100 zlotys, and the cost of a grenade was 10,000 zlotys. The young Jewish fighters – the *de facto* rulers of the ghetto – forcibly taxed everyone in the area to obtain the required funds, especially the remaining few who were rich (i.e., the major smugglers). Most of the jewellery, furs and other expensive items that still remained hidden were poured into the effort.

To make matters even more difficult, once we got our hands on the items we still had to smuggle them into the ghetto. My friends played a key role in this. Prior to the resistance they had just been food smugglers; now they were also bringing in arms.

On 18 January 1943, the Germans marched in for their second Aktion. The ghetto was blockaded early in the morning. Then the German units and support troops penetrated. For the most part, the Jews still didn't have enough guns or ammunition to put up mass resistance. However, there was a little, and that was important because it was the first time the Germans had encountered any, and it was enough to keep them off balance. They were no longer marching into the ghetto with smiles on their faces expecting easy work.

What frustrated them most was that the Jews were hiding. For weeks, people had been gathering in hidden attics and cellars, and the Germans were hesitant to enter these for fear of being ambushed.

The Nazis had wanted to round up 8,000 people in a one-day effort. However, they only captured 3,000 that first day, and had to return over the next few days when they could only catch 2,000 more. They also killed about 1,000 Jews in the streets – in retaliation for the 70 Germans we killed or injured.

Once they left, we knew the battle had just begun, and that they would be back with increased force to finish off what remained of the ghetto. But we would be ready. The Nazis were going to have a battle on their hands if they wanted to send the rest of the 35,000 Jews off to slaughter. We were going to make our mark in history.

From February to April 1943 the main activities of the ghetto focused on our hiding places. In January Jews had generally concealed themselves in attics and cellars – improvised arrangements. After the Aktion, there was a concerted effort to build elaborate bunkers – subterranean shelters designed to sustain many people for long periods of time.

Throughout April, there were persistent rumours of a German incursion, and people were ready to go to their bunkers at a moment's notice. Most of this was taking place while I was on the Aryan side with my brother. However, I was still making frequent trips into the ghetto, so I was aware that the resistance efforts were underway. In fact, I was there for the most famous moment in the ghetto's history.

On 18 April, I had come into the ghetto to deliver special Passover treats to my smuggling friends. That day, the ghetto received reports the Germans were congregating in massive numbers. In response, we reinforced our look-out posts that had been set up throughout the area. We confirmed the mobilization, and readied ourselves for an attack. The Germans were unaware of how prepared we were.

For once I was actually looking forward to the enemy coming into the ghetto. I had a sense that I was about to witness an historic day that Jewish children would learn about for centuries to come.

I must admit that I really didn't know much of the specifics of our resistance. The most important planning was done in total secrecy, and I was just an 11-year-old boy who, from the fighters' perspective, didn't need to know too much. But my smuggling life got me in close enough contact with some of the Jewish Fighting Organization (JFO) that I had a sense of what was happening. I was enthusiastic to do whatever I could to help the cause, and occasionally I was used as a messenger boy. I was sent from one section of the ghetto to another, delivering different weapons to various groups.

Most of the fighters were young adults – I figure the whole group of them were in their twenties or early thirties. They were extremely impressive – heroic men and women ready to die with honour. Their leader was Mordecai Anielewicz, then only in his early twenties. The headquarters of the movement was 18 Mila.

I never met Anielewicz, but there were four big-time fighters whom I had come to know quite well. They were among the ghetto's major smugglers – bringing wagons of food through the gates past guards they had bribed. Whenever I had to stay over in the ghetto they fed me and let me sleep at their home – if you can call it that, because it consisted of little more than a few smelly mattresses and boxes. But it was safe there, and that was all that mattered.

I suppose you could say I was their pet. I would always bring them small treats they specifically asked for – usually delicatessen items such as sausages. That was what I had brought them for Passover.

Their names were Szlojme, Jacob, Aaron and Jankiel Kleinman – I remember his last name because of the similarity to mine. I admired him the most – a large man who was the leader of the gang. He was a rough-and-tumble character, but he had a heart of gold.

They also had two women with them – Zlata and 'Florida' – to do their cleaning and cooking, and to be sexual partners. I couldn't understand why they called the older woman Florida, so I asked one of the men one day. He told me they gave her that name because 'a lot of ships sailed into her'. 'Get the picture Jankiel?' he asked. As a naïve 11 year-old, I wasn't quite sure what he meant, but I didn't want to look stupid, so I said I understood. I even remember telling him: 'You don't have to draw me a picture to explain it.'

That place was pretty wild. In the daytime, they smuggled and slept. During the night, they boozed heavily, played cards and enjoyed their women. And they didn't restrict themselves to Zlata and Florida. When they would tire of sex with them, they would send me out to a certain address with a note. I would wait a few minutes for a response, and every time the answer would be: 'Yes, they will be there at the requested hour.'

'They' were always pretty young women who prostituted themselves for food. This was their way of surviving. It was an insult to Zlata and Florida – they were even in the room when the men had sex with those other women – but what were they to do? Zlata and Florida had no choice. Where would they stay? How would they eat?

I knew that the men's behaviour was inappropriate at times, but one has to understand that the surreal circumstances of the ghetto changed people. Everyone was certain they were going to die. You really didn't care about anything but living life as fully as you could because you could be dead a minute, an hour or a day later. I liked those men very much and learned a lot from them. Their influence made me a tougher person, and taught me how to confront whatever hardship might come along.

Admittedly, I too was behaving in ways that were unheard of for a boy my age. For instance, I would drink my share of vodka. I often passed out on the floor after a few shots. Of course, I did not drink for the joy of it, but to block out the pain of my existence.

Despite the misery, the anarchy of the situation did result in a few good times too – the best of which involved Zlata. Right from the start, she made quite an impression on me. In contrast to Florida, I thought Zlata was a very sophisticated and intellectual woman.

I had a cold one night when I was staying in the men's apartment. Jankiel told me he had a sure cure for my ailment. When I asked him what that was, he smiled and said I would soon find out. I had just undressed to go to sleep when Jankiel, a little drunk at that point in the night, picked me up off my mattress and took me over to Zlata. Telling her to keep me warm and devise a remedy for my cold, he pulled her blanket back and dropped me right on top of her. She was nude and so was I. It was a bizarre scene and I didn't know how to react. I turned beet-red, feeling extremely awkward and shy lying flesh-to-flesh on top of this 28-year-old woman.

I thought Zlata wouldn't be too keen on the idea but she just laughed and started cuddling me. After a few minutes I began to figure out what was going on, and before I knew it she had slid her hand down into my groin. She asked me if I liked what she was doing. After I told her I did, and she verified it by seeing I had an erection, she laughed and remarked: 'Jankala has an erection. Not bad for an 11-year-old.'

She played with my penis for a while and then whispered in my ear: 'Jankala, would you like to put it in my vagina? I know you are a young little virgin but would you like to play like the big boys?'

'I thought you were just supposed to warm me up,' I said, a little intimidated by this older, beautiful woman. 'Do you not find me attractive enough?' she wondered. I said that was not the case at all. I told her she was very pretty. 'But you're twenty-eight and I'm twelve, don't you think this is weird?' I asked.

'Sooner or later,' she replied, 'you will be with a woman so why not now. You have an erection, so you're certainly capable. And you're not feeling well. This will make you feel better.'

Before I knew it, I had lost my virginity. I didn't know what to think.

After I was finished, I went to the end of the mattress and Jankiel had sex with her for the rest of the evening as I watched. It was very amusing – quite an eye-opener – for an 11-year-old.

Jankiel asked me afterwards if his treatment idea had helped my cold. He said that it was probably 'better than chicken soup'. Sheepishly, I nodded in agreement.

The following morning I asked Zlata why she had sex with me. She said there were two reasons. 'Reason number one is because Mr Jankiel asked me to,' she said. 'And you always do what Mr Jankiel asks. But more importantly, reason number two is that I wanted to introduce you to sex. You deserve to experience the feel of a woman because there's a good chance you'll die before you reach adulthood. You might even die tomorrow, so you should enjoy the warmth of a woman if only once in your young life. And besides, if you do survive, now you have something to look forward to.' I told her I understood what she meant – and that she was as wise as she was beautiful. I asked her why I always had to bring other women when the men already had her and Florida. 'Doesn't that upset you?' I asked.

'They like variety,' she said. 'I guess we can only keep them partly satisfied. They have enormous appetites for women. I don't really mind. I can get my rest when they're with those other women. I can't believe I'm saying these things to you,' she added. 'You're just a kid.'

'I wasn't a kid last night,' I said, and then hinted towards seeing if we could do it again. 'You little devil!!! Let's just leave it at this one time,' she said sternly but politely. I changed the subject right away. She was so nice to me I wasn't going to do anything to upset her. She never raised the subject again, and never let me touch her again. However, when I was with the men, I would refer to the experience as a way of showing them that I was a man just like them. Of course, I was serious, but I think they just found it cute.

Looking back on it today, I still think she was absolutely correct in her reasons for having had intercourse with me. When you could die any minute, you took what you could out of life and made the most of it. That woman taught me a lot and helped me grow up before my time. I will never forget her. She was a very special person.

Jankiel and his friends were also very special to me. I can still vividly recall their hardy, battle-toughened faces. They were fiercely dedicated to their cause and that dedication kept them going. They worked secretly, trusting only those they knew were as committed. They attended secret meetings where details of uprising attacks were worked out.

I was staying with Jankiel's gang that anxious night of 18 April. With all the activity around the ghetto walls, I wasn't going anywhere. Very early in the morning of the 19th, the Germans marched in. We were all asleep when we heard a knock at the door.

'Wake up, wake up,' a man yelled as loud as he could. 'The swines are marching into the ghetto. Hurry, hurry to the hiding place.' We scrambled to 51 Mila – the third house from the corner of Mila and Lubetska.

When we got there Jankiel told the two women and me that we'd be staying at the hiding place without them. They said they were going to fight, and that we'd probably never see them again. They hugged us goodbye, reached for their guns, and ran off to do battle. I wanted to go with them, but they wouldn't let me – literally shoving me firmly into the hiding place.

Because of the first Aktion, I had experience with hidden attics and secret rooms. But this place was different; I had no idea a place like it could even exist. It was such a well-planned space. There were three large rooms into which about a hundred people could fit. There were even some bunk beds, a water supply (a 20-foot-deep well), and some food which was to be shared by everyone. Within five minutes, it was filled and the trapdoor leading to it was shut. One pleasant surprise when I got there was that I saw that my friend Sevek had also been led into the room. We hadn't seen each other in a long time, so we were happy to meet up again – even if it was under such stressful circumstances.

Outside the bunker, we could hear the German army marching into the ghetto. Everyone stayed totally quiet. That was our only chance of staying undetected. After an hour or so, we heard the sounds of battle, but we weren't sure what was going on. I had wished I was out with the men to see it with my own eyes.

We later found out that the Germans entered the ghetto in two columns. Jewish combat forces were settled high up in buildings in a few different locations. They had a system established in which they could move from rooftop to rooftop, thereby avoiding the danger of the streets.

One clash took place on Nalewki Street, where bombs and hand grenades sent the Germans scrambling in shock and retreat. There was another battle at Zamenhofa and Gesia, which was the site of the main German Command-post for the operation. A third confrontation was at the brush factory. In all cases – even when the Germans regrouped and re-entered more prepared – the Jewish fighters had the advantage of cover, while the Germans were exposed. That first day saw a clear Jewish victory – with only one dead fighter, while the Germans had a few deaths and many casualties.

A few Jewish fighters showed up in our bunker, some looking like professional soldiers because they had grabbed automatic weapons, ammunition and helmets from fallen Germans. It truly was a time to rejoice. There was a wonderful feeling of empowerment for all of us to savour.

So many courageous young people were taking part in the uprising – women as well as men. I remember one of the people who dropped into our hideout was a woman who seemed particularly stoic. She was proudly wearing a German helmet. I asked her where she got it. 'This is a souvenir of a stinking Nazi I killed,' she said. 'I grabbed his gun and his helmet.' I asked her if I could kiss her on her cheek for her bravery. Laughing, she granted me permission. I grasped her hand and told her I hoped she would survive the war and save that helmet to show her grandchildren one day.

I could see the tears forming in her eyes. 'I don't think so,' she said. 'I don't think I will ever see that day. I'm ready to die any time, at any moment, and I'm happy that I was able to be a part of this movement to take revenge on the Nazis.' I knew they were preparing for another attack so I wished her well and told her to come back in one piece. She never returned. When I heard the news it felt as if a knife was being put through my chest. She was one of five young fighters who had died while inflicting heavy casualties on a German Command-post. That woman represented the essence of our movement. She was a brave young person who died with honour and dignity.

She and everyone else knew that our early success may have startled the Germans, but it wasn't going to deter them. They were going to do whatever it took to get the job done, no matter how many men and weapons it required. Our side, meanwhile, only had so much weaponry – much of it of limited use. How good is a revolver when your enemy has a howitzer?

Over those next couple of days, the ghetto transformed into an ugly war zone. The Germans became particularly vicious. Pregnant women were tortured, and mothers had their babies snatched from their arms and had to watch as soldiers saved bullets by bashing the children's heads against the wall. The tide was starting seriously to turn against us. We were dying by the hundreds, but at least many of those victims left this earth with smiles on their faces, proud of their ability to resist.

Initially, the Germans believed we only had a few bunkers. But as the operation continued, they figured out that the ghetto was full of them. As a result, special tactics such as using listening devices and police dogs were used to find our hiding places. These were only modestly successful for them. For instance, we had chemicals to try to throw the dogs off our trail. Clearly, the most effective method for the Germans was the use of Jewish informers – and that is how my hideout was uncovered on 21 April.

As I was sitting quietly with the other hundred or so

people, we heard voices outside and knew the Germans were getting closer. A baby was crying and his mother could not get him to be quiet, so the man in charge of the shelter grabbed the infant from his mother's arms and choked him to death with a cushion. It was cruel, but it had to be done. There were 100 other lives in jeopardy because of the crying. When the mother realized her baby was dead, she started to cry so they knocked her out with a blow to the face before she became too loud.

A short while later, we noticed that the Germans were above us. Then, all of a sudden, we heard our trapdoor ripped away. The Germans began to shout: *'Raus, raus Juden.'* They said we had five minutes to come out, or they would throw grenades and flame-throwers inside and we would all 'die by being burned to a crisp'.

We knew that was not an empty threat. To combat our hidden locations, the Germans concluded that they would destroy every building in the ghetto. This, they thought, could assure the surrender or instant death of every Jewish inhabitant.

So they set about turning the ghetto into an inferno, unleashing the force of heavy artillery including flame-throwers. Many people were burned alive. Others jumped from windows to their deaths. Being underground, we had no windows to jump from, or most of us would have leapt.

Rather than coming in after us, the Germans used the threat of fire to flush us out. I think they stayed back for fear that the bunker was booby-trapped with explosives or that we had guns. But we had neither. All our fighters were outside fighting. We were just hiding, so it wasn't surprising that moments after the German order, the vast majority of the people from the bunker rushed out in a panic with their hands up in the air. People were shaking with fear. Women and children were crying and screaming uncontrollably. Many were disillusioned. 'Where are all the fighters? Where are our heroes?' I could hear one person yell.

In the meantime, I didn't move out with all those people. I was among the minority who was using the full five minutes to choose his or her fate. Each person remaining in that bunker had a difficult decision to make – surrender or burn to death right there.

All of us in that small group decided to stay. I was sitting next to a woman named Frieda. She had two teenage daughters with her and told me she preferred to die there. 'What the hell. I'm going to die with the kids on the outside, so why not die right here instantly? Are you staying Jankiel?' she asked.

I had made up my mind to stay with them. I was a small boy and I knew the Germans would dispose of me – probably on the spot with a bullet to the head. I figured staying put would be a faster and more dignified death.

They then gave us one more warning – that we had two minutes to come out. At that point, my friend Sevek tried to convince me that Frieda was wrong. He said that the bunker meant certain death, but on the outside – no matter how slim – at least there was a chance at survival.

'Jankiel,' he said, 'listen to me. On the outside we can run away while being led to the trains. If you stay here, you'll be dead within half an hour. As bad as it is, give life a chance.' He reminded me it would only be a matter of two minutes before we would be burned to death. That sent shivers down my spine. In the end, I couldn't stomach the thought of dying that way. I kissed Frieda and her daughters goodbye and made my way out of the bunker with Sevek.

Luck was on our side because no one else came with us, and it had been a couple of minutes since the initial wave of people had emerged. We approached the exit and poked our heads out to see if any Germans were around. For their safety, in case any of us had weapons, they weren't right on top of the shelter. They were just outside the building, busily 'processing' the people (i.e., searching for any valuables) who had already climbed out of our bunker. The Nazis were yelling at the people: 'If you do not give us everything you have, you will be shot on the spot. You won't ever see the labour camps.'

The plunderers' preoccupying greed gave me the precious seconds I needed to get away. Barefooted to keep us as quiet as possible, I climbed out behind Sevek. I stepped on a rusty nail as we got out and my foot started to bleed profusely.

I did not even bother to look at my injury – or any of what was happening around me. All I wanted to do was run. It was as though a higher power persuaded me just to run. I knew there was a very good chance that I would be spotted and shot in the back of the head. I also knew that would have been a fast and painless end – better than being sent to Treblinka or burned to death in that bunker.

As Sevek joined the group being readied for Treblinka, I dashed across the street and was wildly lucky to be undetected. I was in the remains of a house that had just burned down. Among the mud and debris, I saw two dead bodies – a man and a woman. They had both been shot in the head. I laid down next to them in the mud as if I too had been shot dead.

I shivered from the cold dampness. It was a creepy situation; it seemed as if the dead bodies were staring at me. None the less, I wasn't going anywhere until I heard the Germans march off. I tore a piece off my shirt, wrapped it around my foot wound, and stayed quietly still.

With my eyes tightly closed most of the time, I listened intently trying to determine what was happening. I could hear light trucks followed by heavier tanks being brought into the ghetto. Then I could hear artillery shells exploding. The houses of our resistance fighters were being decimated; our men and women were severely outmatched.

I was terrified as I curled up in that mud. 'What am I doing here? If I survive till dark, where am I going to go?' I cried to myself. I wasn't really talking to myself, but to my dead parents. I was looking for their help to get me out of this horrible situation in which I was lying next to two dead bodies and surrounded by a chaotic inferno. If hell is how the Christians have always described it, it must be a much more pleasant place than where I was.

About 30 minutes later, I thought I could hear the Germans marching off into the distance. It was finally safe to open my eyes. Then I got up – wet, cold, and covered in mud. I took a closer look at the two bodies to see if I knew them. I think they were both in their twenties, but it was hard to tell for sure because their faces were so bloodied and disfigured. They must have been two fighters shot during battle. I did not know who they were but I am sure they fought valiantly for our cause.

I ran to a nearby house which wasn't as damaged and figured I could hide in it until dark. I did not know what would happen next. Would I end up just like the corpses I laid next to – shot to death in such a godforsaken inferno? I tried to block those thoughts out of my mind and focus on something positive. I felt that if I could make it through until nightfall, I would go back to our original bunker and see if anyone else was there. I thought that maybe by some miracle someone else had survived.

But no matter how hard I tried, I could not ignore the reality of the situation. I started to cry profusely; it was a release for all that had been building up inside me having witnessed so much tragedy and sorrow in just a few short hours. I began to regret the fact that I was alone, that maybe I should have just died with all the others. I started thinking more about what happened to all those people in our hiding place. Were they really burned to death? Then I thought about the remains of my body had I stayed there. It would just be a charred mess, and there would be no one to bury me. I cried

75

for a few more minutes, but then I regained my composure and made my move towards our hideout. I was too anxious to wait until dark.

I looked both ways for Germans and made a run for it. On the way, I saw a soldier on the other side of the street, so I made a detour into 11 Wolynska – a burned-out apartment building near my old home that I could hide in. At the back of the building I found a laundry tub. I pulled it towards me such that I could peer out above it, but would be hidden from view when I ducked. I felt reasonably safe in this empty building. Its residents must have jumped to their deaths or surrendered themselves.

It was around noon at this point and lying there alone again I could do nothing but think. It was back to the live-or-die dilemma, and death was winning. I wondered what I had really accomplished so far. Had I run away from my friends just so I could die alone a few hours later? At least in the bunker I knew the people and had the comfort of dying in company.

I also started to think again about what would become of my body after death. I thought I would be a hearty meal for the German shepherds or the ghetto's sizable rat population. My mind was racing and, between the intense heat and unmanageable anxiety, my heart felt like an over-worked motor about to explode. I was also dying of thirst. It was so hot in that freshly burned-down building that I had to take all my clothes off.

A few minutes after I arrived, I heard German voices getting closer and closer. Pretty soon they were so near I could hear exactly what they were saying, and I could see everything they did. In fact, at one point I saw a few of them urinate no more than 20 feet from me. I was angry with myself for having left the safety of my spot beside those two dead bodies.

I was terrified, but stayed silent as a mouse and was fortunate to be undetected. A few minutes later, I heard the sound of dishes and saw a big red pot with steam coming out of it. It was time for their lunch, a break from Jew-hunting.

After a while, they finished their meal and left. I stuck my head out for fresh air as relief from the unbearable heat. I was desperate for some water but didn't want to risk walking out of that cellar. There may still have been a guard or two there so this time I demonstrated patience and waited until dark.

As I lay there all afternoon, I continued to hear lots of shooting, explosions and artillery fire. I was hoping that the Germans were at least also suffering a few casualties during those battles.

Darkness finally neared, so I got dressed into my dried clothes, looked carefully to see if anyone was nearby, and left the building. I knew the Germans departed for the night; it was to their advantage to work in daylight when they could uncover hiding places and be better prepared for the hit-and-run fighters.

With some high-rise blocks still burning, I headed towards our hideout – the place I had fled at the start of the day. Even though it was just a short walk away, it was a painful one. My foot was severely cut, and the pavement was still hot from all the fire.

When I arrived I could not believe the scene. The first thing I noticed was the unmistakable stench of death. Burnt flesh has a horrendously powerful odour. My disgust was matched by the sight of burnt bodies. All that was left of my friends who chose not to come out was a jumble of bone fragments – barely recognizable body parts. The Germans hadn't just threatened us. They really did torch the place by throwing several grenades in and then setting the building on fire. It was still smouldering.

All alone, I sat down and began hysterically to cry my eyes out. I was doing it for myself and for the friends I had left in the bunker. I thought about Frieda and her two daughters who tried to convince me to stay behind with them – how they were now just burned remains. It made me sick to my stomach. I wanted to vomit, but that was impossible because I had no food in my stomach.

I said a prayer for them, even though I no longer believed in the existence of the Almighty any more. 'If there really was a God, how could he let all this happen?' I thought. All these little children had been slaughtered, and they had never even had a chance to sin – they never even knew what the word meant. Where was God for them? Why had he not struck all the Nazis dead? I was very bitter and very hurt. And the morbid wondering was continuous: when and how was I going to die?

In the midst of my crying, I felt a tap on my shoulder, and leapt with fear. Still wrapped up with all those thoughts of my burned friends, I thought it was a ghost. But when I turned around, I noticed that it was Szlojme, Aaron, Jacob and Jankiel. They could not believe their eyes when they saw me. We embraced with joy.

'How did you get here?' they asked. 'How is it that you're alive and all the others are dead?' I explained what had happened, including the two bodies I hid next to. Then I asked them the same question, and they said they had hid in the sewers while all the destruction was occurring. Realizing how lucky we were to cross paths again, they promised to take me with them wherever they went and not to let me out of their sight. This gave me a feeling of much-needed security.

We said Kaddish for the people from our bunker – the closest we could come to giving them a decent burial, and then we went to where the two fighters had died. My friends searched them for identification. It turned out they were a married couple. Aaron actually knew the man. As tough a man as Aaron was, he seemed extremely shaken by the discovery.

My friends dug a small grave, we said a prayer, put the couple's remains in the ground, and then covered the hole with dirt. I wonder if their bones are still buried there today.

As we prepared to move on, I remember how a part of me envied the charred remains of those soldiers. Their ordeal was over while I was still waiting for my resolution. I couldn't stop thinking about death. I wondered yet again how I would die. Would I be shot? Would I be sent away? Most 11 year-olds were probably concerned with tomorrow's test in school, while I was debating about what form my certain death would take.

With the bodies buried, my friends then took me on what they called a mission. When I asked what it was, they told me I would find out soon enough.

Within an hour, we had tracked down the hiding place of a Jew named Schmool. Earlier that day, he had been seen with the Germans, showing them bunker locations he knew of. My friends confronted this man, who was about their age, yelling at him – calling him a 'rotten traitor' for giving away the locations of seven Jewish hiding places, including the one I was in. In return for his cowardly act, the Germans gave him some food and the promise that his life would be spared. It was well known that the Germans killed all their Jewish informers once they were no longer of any use to them, but it didn't seem to deter some people like Schmool.

My friends told the man he had betrayed them unforgivably. Each pulled out his pistol and fired two shots into the traitor. When they were sure he was dead, they pulled his fancy boots off and threw his body into a cellar, hoping the Germans would find the corpse and get the message. Now that I knew he was the one who had given my hiding place away to the Germans, I wished the men had given me a pistol to help kill him.

My friends told me that the next morning Schmool was to

meet the Germans to reveal more hiding places for more food. Fortunately, we saved a few more lives by killing him before he could do more damage. They took out a bottle of booze and we each had a swig. We left feeling relieved and satisfied with the execution.

It was around 10 p.m. and time to return to their hiding place – a sewer canal at the corner of Lubetska and Mila. It was a disgusting scene – the sewage system was putrid and full of huge rats. The group of us spent a large portion of our time warding them off.

As soon as we arrived we had something to eat – my first meal of the day. The men had kept some food in steel containers for protection against the rats. Our mealtime discussion focused on what had happened in the previous few hours of battle.

'Yes we killed plenty of those bastards,' said Jankiel, 'but not as many as we would have liked. They brought in heavy artillery, tanks and even planes to bomb each and every house on every street in the ghetto. That's why you saw it all ablaze,' he told me.

Now that I had a chance to reflect, I realized how lucky I was – to leave with Sevek, get by undetected, safely hide through the day, and then be found by my friends. Had they not seen me, I don't know what I would have done. My legs were paralysed with fear just thinking about it.

When I went to sleep on my wet and foul-smelling mattress, my thoughts turned to my brother Eli. Not only was I worried about him, but also I realized he would be nervously wondering if I was alive or not. I really wanted to get back out and see him again as soon as possible.

It was clear the Jewish resistance was not going to last much longer. Our numbers were dwindling, ammunition was running out, the ghetto was burning to ashes, and food was scarce. We didn't feel defeated though. We knew from the start that we were no match for the Germans, but to die in battle gave some meaning to inevitable death. They could kill us but they could never take our accomplishments away from the history books.

We realized, however, that it was best at that point to get out of there and try to survive on the Aryan side. We were convinced it would only be a matter of hours before the Germans obliterated us and the rest of ghetto. The sewers were our only haven as the Germans weren't wise to them yet, but that wouldn't last long either.

Although technically the uprising would last for another three weeks, to all intents and purposes it was over. If life was to continue, the only way was to leave the ghetto. The next day – my birthday – we formulated our plans for getting out.

6 • *Three Kilos of Sugar*

We decided our best chance to escape the ghetto was through the sewers. These wound all the way through Warsaw, and we felt that there was probably a route that would take us to a manhole cover that exited on to the Aryan side. Jankiel said it was up to Aaron and me to determine the route.

We figured it was too risky to go during the day so we arranged to conduct our search after dark. Our plan was to spend the night trying to find a path, return to our 'base', and then leave permanently with the others the following night.

Aaron and I set out late in the evening, taking two large candles with us, along with a flashlight to be used sparingly. Before leaving, we made a kind of glue out of flour and water, and cut some refuse paper into small pieces. We used these to create numbered stickers which could be put on the sewer walls to mark where we'd been so we wouldn't get lost – and to provide us with a clear route to follow for the final departure.

The sewers were about three or four feet high. That wasn't much of a problem for me because I was so small – which was why I was chosen for the assignment. But it was a different story for Aaron. Even though he was the youngest and shortest of the four men, he was still close to six feet tall, so his back became extremely sore as the journey progressed. Adding to the unpleasantness, we were up to our eyeballs in smelly raw sewage, and rats were scurrying all around us. It was a disgusting breeding ground for disease.

To take our minds off our situation, and to pass the time more quickly, we talked about all the experiences each of us had been through and friends of ours who had fought in the ghetto battles. Zlata was a large part of that conversation.

Aaron asked me if I knew what happened to her. I told him she was taken away along with the many others in our bunker who had surrendered. I then paused for a moment and added that perhaps she had survived because she was a strong and healthy 28-year-old, and the Germans may have put her to work instead of her sending to the gas chambers. It was a night to be upbeat, as we were hoping to escape, and I didn't want to fill it with negative thoughts. Realistically, however, we both knew that Zlata and all the others shipped off were probably dead by now.

After crawling for about three hours, we finally reached a spot we were quite certain led to a street on the Aryan side. There were about 20 steps to climb up before reaching the manhole cover. I marked the location of that ladder with the three largest stickers, labelled with the words 'Aryan Side'. We could now return to the others, feeling pleased that we had accomplished our mission. By following the markings we had put up along the way, we made it back in about an hour.

When we returned, we told the other men that the only obstacle was removing the manhole cover. Jankiel said he'd need some time to acquire some tools to prise the plate open. Perhaps because of that, or for some other reason unknown to me, he decided that we would leave 48 hours later instead of the next night. The minor delay didn't bother us. We were optimistic about our chances, and looking forward to the journey.

After getting a little rest in the morning, we started the afternoon of our first waiting day by getting organized to leave. Then, late that afternoon, we heard screaming in the distance – and the voices were getting closer. Soon, there was a funny smell in the air.

Just a few blocks away, a Jewish hideout linked to the sewers had been discovered. After saturating the location with gas, and seeing none of the 100 or 200 people there flee, the Germans must have become suspicious, entered the building, and discovered a connection to the underground system. They reacted by pumping massive amounts of gas into the sewer.

As quickly as we could, we dashed ahead of the chased Jews. Unfortunately, our labelled route out of the ghetto would have taken us back toward the fugitives before looping back around to the Aryan side. All our stickers were now useless. We were just scrambling to stay ahead of the oncoming men, women and children.

Within 10 or 15 minutes, we spotted a ladder going up to a street. Arriving there a couple of minutes in advance of the first fleeing Jews, I ran up the metal steps, squeezing beside my friends so each of us could get as close as possible to the manhole lid. Through its tiny holes we took turns breathing fresh air. When all the others made it to our spot, they wanted to climb up and breathe too, but there was barely enough air and space for my friends and me. As the terrified Jews struggled to climb the ladder, we instinctively we kicked them down to the ground. It was selfish, but when you're fighting for survival you just react and do whatever is required.

With the concentration of gas increasing, it didn't take long for the people under us to start losing consciousness. Moments later we were beginning to feel overcome ourselves. We could not wait any longer so we pushed and pushed and managed to flip open the cover. We jumped out and ran across the street as fast as we could, fully expecting to be shot in the process, but to our amazement there were no Germans around.

Once we crossed the road, my friends said to follow them to one or two hideouts nearby. They weren't sure whether these were still intact but felt we had no choice but to find out. We went to one just down the street and were relieved that, despite the German attacks, a group of people they knew remained in hiding there. And we were even luckier with

The only remaining photograph of any member of Jankiel's immediate family. His younger brother Eli (left) was killed a few months after this photo was taken in 1943.

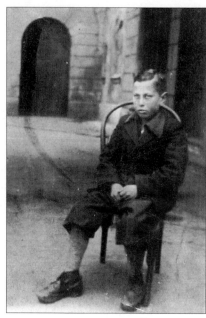

Jankiel at Three Crosses
Square, 1943.

Jankiel (right) with his good friend
Zybyszek, 1943.

Identity card for Jankiel's gentile persona, 'Janek Jankowski', 1944.

Mrs Lodzia,
Jankiel's guardian
angel, 1945.

Mrs Lodzia's two daughters,
Irka (left) and Marysia, 1945.

Jankiel's friend Sevek, having
survived the war, taken in 1950.

Bull, the leader of the cigarette
sellers, 1945.

Lutek, the accordian player, 1950.

Jankiel in 1945 – he learned to play the accordian in post-war Poland.

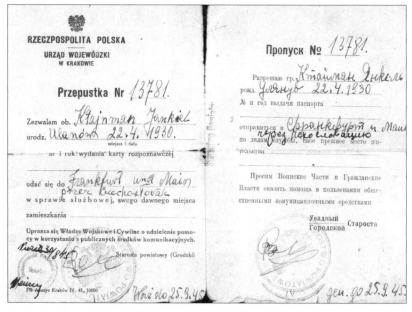

False identity papers used to get Jankiel out of Poland, 1945.

Jankiel, second from the right, with other students at the orphanage in England, 1946.

The Head of Jankiel's orphanage in England, 1946.

Jankiel (right) with three orphanage colleagues and two dogs; the one on the right is 'Queenie', 1946.

Jankiel (Jack) playing the drums after settling in Canada, 1949.

Jack's marriage to Sonia in Israel, 1959.

some remarkable timing. The group there of about 25 people was getting ready to leave the ghetto that night, having arranged for two Poles who worked in the sewers to lead them out. Each night, after the Germans left the ghetto for the day, these two men would take a group of Jews out to the other side.

Around 11 p.m. that night, all of us waited at a designated spot a few blocks away, hoping for the sewer workers to show up. A short while later, a tall thin Polish man arrived. Having already travelled through the sewer to get to us, he looked like a big banana in his yellow rubber boots and overalls. 'Let's go,' he said. 'Whoever is ready, we're going now. Make sure you have your payments ready.'

This was news to me – and sent a shiver down my spine. I should have known profit was the only reason they would help Jews. The fee was 5,000 zlotys, or an equivalent amount in gold or jewellery. All I had was my little bag filled with candles from our sticker-making trip. I think he assumed the sack was filled with valuables, and I didn't say or do anything that would make him think otherwise. I gripped it as if it was filled with jewels.

As we departed, I went to the front of the line, close behind the sewer man. He must not have had his dinner yet, as he pulled a loaf of bread and a large piece of sausage from his bag. I couldn't help but stare at his food. I was so hungry I would have given my right arm for some of it. He finally got my message, and cut a piece of bread and sausage for me. 'Here,' he yelled – and tossed the food to me. I gobbled it down within seconds. It tasted delicious and gave me energy for the trip ahead.

The arrangement was that we would pay him once he got us to the other side. That was fair, because if we had paid before the trip he could have just taken the money and turned us over to the Germans. We set off, and I remained right behind the man's rubber pants. He was familiar with the sewers so he moved very quickly. The few of us at the front could keep up, but most of the group had difficulty. We had to stop several times and wait for them to catch up.

About 30 minutes later, we arrived at the ladder that led to the Aryan side. Just before I was to climb out, the sewer worker demanded payment from me. Rather than give him my bag, I told him that my father was among those at the back of the group, and he would pay for me when he caught up to us. The man gave me a strange look, but said that was OK as long as I stayed near him until my father showed up. The man then began collecting payment from the others as they arrived. As soon as they paid him, they'd go up the ladder.

A few minutes later, when he had six to eight people to deal with, he seemed to forget about me, so I went up the stairs with those who had just paid. After climbing about 20 steps, we were at street level where another Polish man was waiting to pull us out. It was well after curfew, so he was risking his life to be there. But the risk was minimized by having chosen a quiet, dead-end street that was likely to be unpatrolled.

Once on the street, the Jews just stood there quietly, waiting for all the others to arrive, when they were all to be led off by the workers. At that point I decided to run for my life. I couldn't take the chance that the worker would see me again and demand payment. It was the last I saw of any of those people – including my four friends.

I ran for a few blocks until I came to a large apartment building that looked inviting. I quietly entered the lobby and noticed that there was a washroom. It had about 12 toilet stalls, along with a hose that delivered running water. I smelled like the sewer, so I thoroughly washed myself, and tried to clean my clothes too. I then hid in a stall until morning to ensure I would not be caught after curfew. And it gave my clothes a little time to dry.

As I sat there, all I could think about was seeing Eli again. Just the thought of him made me happy and full of hope, which is something I really needed considering the three days of hell I had just been through.

I left the building a few hours later when the sun rose, and jumped on the tail of a streetcar going to Praga. I arrived at Eli's building and entered the converted stable he was staying in. But he wasn't there. In fact, I looked all over the place and he was nowhere to be found.

I went to visit our landlady to see if she knew where he was. She turned pale as a ghost and said she had bad news for me. She said that a suspicious neighbour had called the police the day before to say a Jewish boy was hiding on her street. When the authorities came, she said, they approached her demanding to know the truth. She told them she had no idea what they were talking about, but that if a Jew was staying on her property, it was without her knowledge, and she agreed he should be caught.

Apparently, Eli had seen them coming and while they were talking to the landlady he fled to the cellar of another house. However, someone saw him do this and informed the policemen.

I was told they approached the cellar with their guns drawn – as though Eli was some kind of dangerous gangster. All they found was a frightened little boy curled up in a corner crying his eyes out. The men pulled my little brother out by his long blond hair and started beating him with their sticks. I was told they savagely pounded him, even though he offered no resistance. All he did was repeatedly call out my name: 'Janek, Janek, help me. Where are you? Help me."

I don't know what they ended up doing with him. I'm not sure whether they shot him, tortured him, or sent him away to a death camp. All I know is that he was never heard of again. I tried to identify who called the police but could not learn anything more than that it was a woman resident of that street. Had I found out who it was, I was enraged enough to get a gun and shoot the heartless scum. I would have gladly traded my life to take revenge on the person responsible.

It was frustrating to be told that all the neighbours had gathered to watch the incident. How could the people who witnessed the episode not feel sorry for the little boy and do something to help? These people who watched had children of their own, and the two policemen may have had children as well. How could they be so cruel? At least the landlady had the decency to tell me what happened, and did not turn me in, even though by this time she knew for certain I was Jewish.

The whole time I was in the ghetto, I was more worried about myself than Eli. After all, he was on the outside, and in a protected location. When we had found that place, I thought it would be a safe haven. I really believed it gave him a good chance of surviving the war – an opportunity to grow up and become a special young man. Thanks to the barbarity of the Germans and the Poles, he never got the chance. I again learned the lesson that in Warsaw there was no such thing as safety for a Jew.

All Eli and I really had in life was each other. I hate to imagine how he must have felt when he cried out for me – the only person on this cruel earth who could help him – only to be left on his own, sentenced to a painful death. I felt sick to my stomach. The war was making me witness the very worst of humanity; there was no end to the ruthlessness.

The reality was that Eli lost his life over three kilos of sugar – the reward received by that despicable neighbour who turned him over to the authorities.

At first I felt guilty, thinking that had I not been involved in the uprising perhaps I could have saved my brother. On the other hand, I realized that I too would have been taken away – though at least we would have died together.

Eli and I were all that was left of what once was a large family. We understood that as long as we had each other, we still had a sense of family and, with it, a shred of normality in life. So many times when I wanted to die it was the thought of Eli that kept me going. Losing him was the hardest blow of all.

To add to the torment, it happened just after my 12th birthday. What a present – nothing but tragedy and sorrow. Tears kept welling up in my eyes. I wondered how much more I could take. I was now truly alone. The way I felt, I could have taken my own life, but somehow I found the motivation to survive. I decided that keeping the family name alive and telling the world what the Nazis had done to Eli and my family was enough incentive to keep living.

And I did have a glimmer of hope. At least I was on the Aryan side so, for the moment anyway, I had a chance to keep going. As with all the deaths of people close to me, there was no time to mourn. I had to focus on surviving – and at that moment remained alert enough to know that I had to flee that place immediately. I realized the same person who gave my brother away could call the police and have me taken away as well.

I left for Saska Kepa – a different neighbourhood a few miles away where my friends Pavel, Zenek and Zybyszek operated. With a heavy heart, I went back to what I knew best. I knocked on some doors in a rich neighbourhood and started begging; I got some bread and a little meat. I had no appetite but I knew my stomach needed some food in it. Even with such sorrow, you have to eat if you want to have any hope of surviving.

The first few nights after Eli died were emotionally devastating. It was early springtime, warm enough that I could sleep in the park and other outdoor sites. I would cry myself to sleep, thinking constantly about how much I missed my brother. I still don't know how I managed to stay sane.

Slowly but surely, I got myself back into the rhythm of survival. I obtained a new cross to wear around my neck and resumed my tried-and-true begging-and-singing method. And once again, I experienced my share of adventures.

One warm night I chose to sleep in the local amusement park that had closed for the night. I found a swinging ride with two or three compartments, each designed to hold two people. It seemed to be a safe, quiet and relatively comfortable place to spend the night.

About half-an-hour after settling down I heard footsteps approaching the ride. I had to hide, and fortunately was small enough to be totally concealed after climbing under the two-person seat in my compartment. As the voices came nearer, I could hear that it was a man and a woman, both speaking German. It seemed they worked together in an office and were on a date. Without lifting my head, I stayed motionless, waiting for them to finish their discussion and leave. But they weren't going anywhere. He wanted to make love to her in the swing. She didn't want to but eventually gave in and they came into my compartment.

They proceeded to have intercourse, inches above my head. I was lying flat on my back, getting sick to my stomach as the swing went up and down repeatedly. Soon after they finished the act they left, and I fell asleep – completely exhausted. I was very lucky to get by undetected and never went back there.

The Germans were serious about the 9 p.m. curfew for Warsaw. There were some people who tried to stay out later, but they were very foolish. Jeep patrols drove around all night and when they saw people on the streets they would often shoot first and ask questions later. It didn't matter whether it was two lovebirds or a vagrant child. Many Poles were killed this way.

As I had learned with Eli, the heavily forested park was

usually the most convenient and hassle-free location for sleeping, but I encountered a few scary moments there too. I once shared an area of the park with a Polish couple who, after a dinner date and stroll for fresh air, realized it was too late to get home safely. They shared a bottle of vodka and spent the night making love in the bushes.

I didn't dare sleep that night. Had they come near me to urinate, for example, I could have been discovered and reported. Instead of sleeping, I entertained myself by listening to them all night long. They talked dirty when they had sex, and by listening I was able to add to my vocabulary what must have been every Polish profanity ever uttered.

The park was important for more than just sleeping. It was my bathroom too. On the nights it was cold and not a popular place to be – and usually between 1 and 5 a.m. when it was dark and no one could see me – I would slip into the river and wash myself. Some days I emerged from the river as red as a tomato because the water was so cold, but I felt healthy and strong and didn't let it bother me. I needed that mental toughness. I couldn't allow the cold to affect me because I simply could not afford to get sick. Illness was a death sentence. If I did feel a little under the weather, I convinced myself that I was fine, and just kept going, forcing myself to recover quickly.

On really damp chilly days I came up with creative ways to keep myself warm. For example, the churches were an excellent solution. They always kept their doors open for fine young Catholics. I would enter the church, kneel down, and go through the motions of praying. I learned all the Catholic prayers and even went to services on Sundays. The priests used to like it when I was there, relishing the chance to talk with such a religious youngster.

One time a priest asked where my parents where. I told him my mother was dead and my father was bitter about losing her so he stopped believing in God. This got the priest interested in my life, and he tried hard to become my friend. In fact, he was repeatedly asking questions about my family, so I stopped going to his church. After that, I rotated churches because I did not want to let any priests get to know me too well and start asking personal questions that could reveal my identity.

One day I tried a church run by a man called Father Jan. I quickly realized he was different from the other priests. He was younger and seemed more in tune with regular people. He was friendly, but gave me my space and didn't pressure me with lots of overly personal questions. 'Have you come here to pray because you are so religious?' he asked after letting me kneel alone for most of my first visit. 'Or is it just that this is a place where you can stay warm and dry?'

I told him it was for both reasons. I said that I was a firm believer in Jesus and that I enjoyed praying, but a life on the streets meant I needed to stay dry. 'Is it all right to do so Father?' I asked. 'Is it all right to come in here?'

'My son, come in as many times as you like. It is perfectly all right, perfectly all right.' Had he known I was Jew, I am not sure he would have felt the same way. Maybe he would have, but I was not about to take that chance.

Because I felt more comfortable there than at any of the other churches, I abandoned my rule of not going to one location too often, and made his church a regular part of my routine. I even went to Father Jan for confession on several occasions.

As I came more often, I got to know him better. And over time, he did start to ask more probing questions, but he never went too far. I told him that I lived with an aunt as my parents had died in a traffic accident two years previously, and that I had to beg on the streets to help her pay the bills. When he asked why she never went to church I told him she was an atheist who refused to go, but that I was praying she would have a revelation some day and change her ways. With all the lies I was telling, I suppose it was a good thing we had those confession sessions.

From all I could see, Father Jan seemed to be a good person. Perhaps he had suspicions about whether my story was true, but he never said anything that would make me feel threatened. It was difficult living a lie all the time because I always had to keep my guard up. I had to think carefully before I said anything. All it took was one wrong word to slip out of my mouth. It was hard to stay so alert all the time.

There were a few precious moments when I could partially escape. For instance, I would treat myself to a show once a week or so. For ten cigarettes, I would bribe the doorman at the theatre to let me in.

I would get a bite to snack on and settle into a chair in the empty rows at the front of the theatre. It was two hours of feeling like a normal person – sharing in the same experience as any other theatre-goer. Of course, once the lights came back on it was back to reality. Everyone else had a home to return to while I had to run out of there and search for shelter for the night, always knowing in the back of my mind that I could be caught any time. It was a difficult transition – from the joy of watching the play to the stress of seeking refuge.

One rainy night I was looking for somewhere to sleep and ended up at 5 Radzitowska, site of a four- or five-storey apartment building. Next to its back door was a shed containing eight large rubbish cans. I entered the shed and arranged the containers so that I could lie down behind them and not be seen if someone came in to throw out their rubbish. I stole a straw mat from the doorway of one of the apartments, laid it on the cement as a mattress, and used a large potato bag as a blanket. I went to sleep very late because I was always afraid I might snore and be discovered by a resident who had come to take out their refuse before going to sleep.

Very early the next day – around 6 a.m. – I was awoken by some rustling noises above me. I lay there very quietly, listening intently but unsure exactly what was going on. I was seized with fear. The cans were being put back into their original position, and within a few moments I was exposed and vulnerable. I curled myself up in a ball.

A tall, fortyish woman towered over me. She was the superintendent. 'My God,' she shrieked – thinking at first she had stumbled across a dead body. Reluctantly, I looked up, and she realized I was alive.

'Who are you? What are you doing here? Get up little boy – this is no place for sleeping!' she snapped.

We stared at each other for a moment or two and I began to spin another tale to try and get myself safely out of there. I told her I was a farm-boy from outside Warsaw who wanted to spend a day in the big city. I said I hitchhiked into town, and spent the day touring around. Before long it got late. I explained that I needed a place to sleep for the night, and I had no money for a room so this spot looked as good as any. 'But now that it's morning I'll head back,' I said. 'Sorry if I've caused you any inconvenience.'

This woman looked unimpressed. 'You're not fooling me,' she said, staring me straight in the eye. 'You're a Jewish boy in hiding aren't you? Don't be afraid. Tell me the truth. I won't give you away.'

I told her again that I was a gentile boy. 'Look at my cross,' I said. 'I can recite some prayers for you. Believe me, I'm telling you the truth. I'm not a Jew.' But she wouldn't let the issue rest.

'You'd better be honest with me,' she said. 'Are you really a Jewish boy? If you'll just tell me the truth, I'll let you sleep there as long as you want. I don't care. I won't tell anybody. But I demand that you tell me the truth.' I still wouldn't change my story, so she finally dropped the issue and changed the subject.

'All right,' she said, 'whatever your story is you must be hungry. Why don't you come into my apartment for a bite to eat?'

My head told me it was a trap, and that maybe I should just make a run for it. But I was hungry and for some reason I took the risk, following her into the building. She had a very modest flat – a bathroom and one main room, which had space for not much more than a couple of beds, a few kitchen appliances and a table.

The woman offered me a cup of hot chocolate. She also gave me some bread and butter. 'I bet you didn't have much to eat yesterday,' she said. I insisted that was not true – but it was difficult to hide how anxious I was to eat.

I changed the subject, asking if she lived there alone. She said she had two teenage daughters, but now that summer holidays had begun they were both away at their grandmother's farm. They would be back in ten days, she said. I asked if her husband was with the girls. 'No, we are separated,' she reluctantly acknowledged. I apologized for asking that question which seemed to upset her.

'Don't feel bad,' she said. 'He's been gone for over three years now. I'm used to it. I just feel sorry for my daughters who have to grow up without a father. That is a shame. Otherwise, I don't miss him at all. He's not really worth talking about. He was an abusive, alcoholic husband.'

Then she paused for a moment before she went too far. 'I don't know why I'm telling you all this. I have just found you among rubbish cans and here I am telling you my most personal details – and you're what – maybe 12 years old.' I told her she had guessed my age exactly.

As our conversation went on, it became clear to me that she was a genuine, good person. She had been so honest with me I finally decided to trust her and reciprocate. 'Well, now that you have told me all about you I will tell you the truth about me,' I said, worried that I might be making a big mistake.

I admitted that I was a Jewish boy, who had lost his whole family – the sole survivor among some 100 relatives. I was crying as I told her about my parents' deaths in the ghetto, how Brenda and Menashe were taken away to the concentration camps, and how I had just lost Eli. I described how I lived on the streets – surviving from day to day, but knowing that I could die at any moment.

She started to cry with me, and gave me a big affectionate hug. It was as though she could feel my pain, as a mother would feel for a child. She kept repeating over and over again what a tragedy my life was. 'This is what Hitler has brought to our country,' she said. 'He's ruined it for all of us, though I know we've got it a lot better than your people.'

My instincts sensed that this woman was genuine. She had become so emotional listening to me. I had strict rules about not trusting anyone, but in this case I felt compelled to make an exception. Looking into her eyes, I could tell she wasn't tricking me; she was different from everyone else. It seemed she really did care for me.

We talked for a couple of hours as I told her all the details about what had happened to me, and at the end of the conversation we exchanged names. I told her that my real name was Jankiel, but that I had to go by the name of Janek in order to survive. Her name was Mrs Lodzia. Her absent daughters were called Irka, who was 15, and Marysia who was 13.

Mrs Lodzia was quite poor, making just enough to support her family in their small apartment. In fact, to make ends meet she needed to do the rich tenants' laundry and ironing.

As I was getting ready to leave, she grabbed me by the arm and said to wait a minute. She went to the bathroom and turned the water on to fill the tub. She said I was dirty and should clean myself up. I was thrilled by the idea. The hot and soapy water felt luxurious; I couldn't remember the last time I had taken a real bath.

After I dried off, she said she wanted to help me on a permanent basis. She insisted that I sleep in her home. 'You realize that the penalty for hiding a Jew is death,' I said. She said she didn't care.

'What about your two daughters?' I asked. 'What if they disapprove?'

'They won't be back for ten days,' she said. 'We'll worry about that later.'

I was stunned at her compassion, and all I could do was thank her repeatedly. 'If only everyone was like you. What a place the world would be. There would be no wars – only happiness. You are such a wonderful person,' I said.

The plan was that I would continue with my normal activities on the streets during the day. At night, I would come 'home' to Mrs Lodzia's to sleep under the kitchen table. It was located right by the window, and because we were on the ground floor and the window opened on to an alley leading to a street, I could quickly escape if a policeman came knocking late at night. I slept in my clothes in case that happened.

Things went really well for the next week and a half, and she was consistently kind towards me. When her daughters came home from the farm, however, they were in for a disquieting shock. They walked in the door and there I was. 'Who is this?' they asked in unison. 'Who is this boy and what is he doing here?' Their mother told them to sit down and she would explain. 'This is Janek. He is Jewish and is the last survivor of his family. I feel nothing but pity for him and I believe you should too. We should all help him.'

'But you know what the posters say,' Irka said. 'If you harbour a Jew the whole family will be shot.'

'Yes, I know about that,' her mother replied. 'But does he look Jewish to you? He looks as gentile as us. And if anyone asks we'll say he's a cousin from the farm and that he's just staying for a few days. Then he'll leave and that will be that.

But for now, it's important we do what we can for him, and that no one knows our secret.' Within a couple of minutes they changed their minds and fully supported their mother's decision to let me stay there.

In fact, I became a good friend to the girls – as though they were my older sisters and I was the brother they never had. I remember one time Mrs Lodzia had to visit her mother for a few days, which she did from time to time, leaving Irka in charge of things, including responsibility for all the superintendent chores.

With Mrs Lodzia away, Irka and Marysia decided to have some fun one night. After I said goodnight to them and crawled under the table, I heard some whispering and giggling. Then Irka said to me: 'How would you like to come and sleep with us? You could snuggle into this nice warm bed right between us. Why don't you go and wash yourself and climb in with us? It will be much nicer than sleeping on the floor.'

I told her I couldn't do that – that her mother would not approve. I said she was trusting us to behave while she was away and she would kick me out if she found out. 'Oh Janek, don't be such a bore. Mother will never know,' she said. 'We give you our word we will not say anything.'

I repeated that I would love to do it, but I just couldn't take the chance. I argued that they might get angry with me sometime in the future and tell their mother about the incident in the heat of the moment. They thought that was nonsense, and said they'd make me change my mind. They literally held me down and undressed me – not that I was resisting too much. Then they 'forced' me to climb into bed with them.

I slept with them for three consecutive nights. Each night I was the perfect gentleman, never touching either of them inappropriately. It was just a fun 'family' thing to do – and it was so nice to sleep in a bed for the first time in ages. I thanked them for a very special memory.

My life in that household had many interesting days. It seemed something unusual occurred whenever someone was at the grandmother's farm. One time when the kids were away for a weekend I was exposed to quite a different side of Mrs Lodzia.

For a short while, she had been seeing a married man who owned a grocery store. They had a quiet, not-so-serious affair going – never appearing together in public, and he would only come over occasionally. With the girls away, he came by unexpectedly one evening while I was in the apartment. When Mrs Lodzia heard the knock at the door she thought it was a tenant and told me to hide behind the curtains where her clothes were hanging.

'How are you stranger?' I heard him ask as she opened the door. 'I apologize for showing up unannounced but I had a yearning for you and I've come with some vodka and goodies, so maybe we can spend some time together.'

She invited him in. I was still hidden and had to keep very quiet, which meant I couldn't let myself fall asleep and risk snoring. I kept myself awake by focusing on the lovemaking, just as I had done weeks earlier in the park. I could see the shadows of their movements, and hear every word they spoke. He would tell her what a wonderful body she had, and how she was so much more attractive than his fat wife. It was amusing and educational stuff, but it was exhausting forcing myself to remain awake and keep so still and quiet for several hours. He finally left, late into the night, and I emerged from hiding.

'Well, now you know everything about me,' she said, 'even my private life.' I think she was embarrassed by my presence though she never appeared to let it inhibit her. All she said was that one day, I would 'understand that a woman needs a man just as a man needs a woman'.

I thought she was worried about what I was thinking, so I told her there was no way I'd lose respect for her just because she had a man over to fill some lonely hours. I told her that now that I knew all the intimate details of her sex life, it was only fair that I tell her mine, and I recounted my experience with Zlata.

'You little devil,' she responded, though a lasting, wide smile said much more than her words. She had a little vodka left over from her night with that man, and we savoured the moment by sharing a toast, along with a piece of expensive and delicious Polish sausage that also remained. Her relationship with the grocer ended soon after – the man's wife was starting to get suspicious so it stopped at nothing more than a quick fling.

I remember one other time seeing Mrs Lodzia in an unexpected light. I was looking for her one hot summer day and knew that if she was not in the apartment she was very likely in the attic doing some laundry. I ran up there and found the door locked. I knocked and told her it was me so she invited me in.

I was shocked to see that she was stark naked. Almost as remarkable as the sight itself was the fact that she didn't seem to care. She could have put her clothes on and then let me in, but I suppose she couldn't be bothered. Maybe she thought this was nothing compared to having watched her have sex.

'Janek, you see these legs,' she said to me. 'I hope men turn their heads at them. What do you think? Are these legs nice?' She may have been fishing for a compliment, but she deserved one. She was about five foot, ten inches tall, blond, and possessed a good body that would indeed turn a good many heads.

'Yes, Mrs Lodzia, they are beautiful and you have a gorgeous figure to go with them. And I might add you have a friendly and pretty face.'

I could not understand how that husband of hers could

have been so stupid as to lose such a beautiful and caring woman with two delightful daughters. I told her that if I were to survive the war and grow into manhood, I would try to be so lucky as to find a woman as insightful, compassionate and attractive as she was.

'Janek, you are flattering me. We both know that I am fast becoming an old lady,' she laughed. 'But I like and appreciate what you are saying. You have an old head on your shoulders. You know how to make a lady feel good, and that is a good thing, a very good thing. Women like to be complimented, a nice word here and there. It's in their nature. They appreciate it. Remember what I'm telling you. Some day you might be able to put it to good use with some lucky girl.' We had these conversations a few more times. I always enjoyed them, and gained a great deal from her wisdom.

After the terrible period that followed Eli's death, I finally had something to be happy about. Mrs Lodzia was nothing short of a guardian angel. She was, and indeed still is – although she is dead now – a major influence on my life. I can never express in words how lucky I was to have slept in that rubbish shed. I met Mrs Lodzia in mid-1943, when the end of the war was still nowhere in sight. There remained many more challenges on the road to survival, and I know that without Mrs Lodzia I wouldn't have had a chance.

7 • *The Catholic Orphan*

While life with Mrs Lodzia and her daughters brought me great joy, I was also fortunate to have some great friends who were like a family to me. In hustling on the streets, I spent a lot of time with Zybyszek, Pavel and Zenek, the Jewish boys Eli and I had met in 1942. After Eli died they had tried hard to ease my pain by maintaining an upbeat atmosphere. They were true friends, dependable people who I knew really cared for me.

There was something special about being with others who shared my persecution. In fact, I figured the four of us were the only boys who had escaped the ghetto and were still alive. Then one day in the summer of 1943 I discovered that there were others.

I was walking with Pavel when we came across a boy and girl singing under a bridge. The boy looked extremely familiar to me. Within a moment or two I remembered that he was from my family's neighbourhood and his name was Bolus. He recognized me as I recognized him, and we greeted each other with warmth, but in a quiet way so as not to draw attention to ourselves.

'I didn't think there were any other survivors,' he said after we exchanged pleasantries. 'I thought all the Jewish kids left were selling cigarettes in Three Crosses Square.'

Three Crosses Square was right in the heart of the German Quarter. It was tough to believe that any other Jewish children could be alive, let alone interacting with German soldiers. I told Bolus I didn't believe him, adding that he shouldn't joke about such a serious matter. But he insisted he was telling the truth, and said we could meet them if we wanted.

The next day a rendezvous was arranged at Three Crosses Square where we would be introduced to the rest of these children.

It turned out that Bolus wasn't lying. There were about a dozen young Jewish boys selling cigarettes in the area. From the moment we exchanged greetings it seemed as if we had known each other all our lives. Perhaps misery loves company, but despite the varying ages and personality differences among the group we all hit it off quite well, and it was a significant morale boost to become a member of this larger group.

The leader of the gang was a boy named Irving – known to everyone as Bull, a strong character who was a few years older than me. Others in the group included Conky, so-named for his big nose, two boys named Stasiek – one was called 'Golec' and the other 'Little Stasiek' – and an extremely handsome young man with a great big smile named Romek.

Almost immediately Zybyszek, Pavel, Zenek and I began selling cigarettes with all the other boys at Three Crosses Square. It was hard work, but no more difficult than the begging we had been doing and far more lucrative.

On profitable days I was able to bring something special back for Mrs Lodzia. For example, I sometimes dealt with Hungarian soldiers, who gave me access to Hungarian cigarettes – far superior to the Polish products – as well as sardines and occasionally a good bottle of wine or brandy. Whenever I got my hands on those or any other uncommon items I brought them back to her apartment and we all shared in the treat.

There were also other benefits to my association with the cigarette sellers. One was the acquisition of false identity papers. I was finally able to document the existence of Janek Jankowski. Irving was connected to the Jewish underground, which had papers made up for all of us. Those documents gave us a much-needed security blanket.

While Irving was dealing closely with those adults, the only Jewish grown-up I had regular contact with was a gentleman we called the 'Amchu Man'. He was in his late thirties or early forties and managed to survive in the most incredible way. He had dug a hole in the ground in a bushy field not far from our neighbourhood. It was very similar to a grave. He covered it with a board, on top of which he laid some soil. He just left a tiny opening for air and light.

Like a nocturnal animal Amchu Man would emerge after curfew and look for food in rubbish cans – risking his life if he'd been caught by the night patrols. He had no choice though. His Jewish appearance would probably have led to him being picked up within minutes of showing his face in public during the day.

To help him, I used to go to the gas company where the workers would get cheap meals in a subsidized cafeteria. I came with two empty cans, and asked if leftovers could be poured into them. They often pitied me and gave me the soup, and as soon as they did I would run over to the Amchu Man and give him one can while I consumed the contents of the other. Amchu Man was able to enjoy more than just the soup on those occasions. I was someone to talk to – and when one is living literally in a hole in the ground that can help you stay sane. In talking to him, I learned that he had lost his wife and children at the Dachau death camp. He was on his way there too but somehow managed to jump off the train. He ended up in Saska Kepa, and had been hiding underground for months since escaping.

My friendship with the Amchu Man and my cigarette-selling friends contributed towards a stronger structure for my life in late 1943. I had a home, a place to work, and little by little the Germans were losing the war. Survival actually seemed possible.

Perhaps I became too confident and cocky as life started to

improve, because I made a few serious mistakes at that time. One involved this elderly woman on Grochowska Street. I had known her since Eli and I stayed with the Slawcias on that street. This woman, who must have been close to eighty, was a close friend of the couple, so she knew we were Jewish but kept the information to herself.

Sometimes I would drop by to visit. She would give me some food, and every now and then I would bring her a gift. She was an extremely religious Catholic, and would entertain me with long sermons – it was almost as if she was some kind of prophet. Once she gave me a long speech about the Old Testament and how it was more important than the New Testament. She said that the Jews were God's chosen people and that despite what was happening in the war they would be the last people left standing on the earth when it came to an end. Another time she told me that God was going to punish the Nazis and the Jews would get their revenge. I found her speeches to be very uplifting. Whether they were true or not was another matter, but they certainly made me feel good.

A few times she let us play with her teenage grandson and granddaughter who would be visiting. One time, she left them alone with another Jewish friend and me, and we all decided to play poker. Within an hour, the girl lost all her money but wanted to stay in the game. Her brother told her the only solution was to pay us 'in other ways' to earn the necessary zlotys to keep playing. She could have quit to avoid the humiliation, but instead insisted on doing whatever was required to continue.

Because I was the 'experienced' one, I went into the other room with her in exchange for a few zlotys. When we resumed playing, she lost those quickly and then my friend took his turn. She lost again, and then went away crying. We had behaved horribly – I wouldn't go so far as to say we were rapists, but we demonstrated our immaturity. We left in a hurry. Although the girl's brother was a jerk who thought the whole thing was a joke, I was worried about repercussions from the rest of their family and never risked returning to that street. I am still sorry for what we did to that girl.

Not long after that experience I made another big mistake that almost cost me my life. By working daily in Three Crosses Square I got to know a few Polish youths who hung out there. In particular, there were two boys who became good friends of mine. They were among the precious few gentiles who knew I was Jewish. I came to trust them after I discovered they were very sympathetic to the plight of the Jews. In fact, their father helped several Jews during the war. The only problem with these boys was that they were extremely wild, and in that sense were a bad influence on me.

One day when Mrs Lodzia was away and I was alone with the girls I ill advisedly invited the boys to drop by our apartment. They arrived in a very hyped-up state, telling me about a German soldier who had raped a Polish woman and her daughter. The two women were friends of the boys' family, and the brothers said they couldn't let the crime go unpunished. They described how they had found out that he was in a local bar so they went there and waited for him to come out. When he emerged half-drunk they followed him home. On the way, they cornered him in alley and shot him twice in the leg with a German pistol.

How they got that gun I'll never know – but there it was. They had brought it over to show me. The weapon was loaded when they put it in my hands. I was trembling as I gripped it. I said I was afraid of killing someone but they just laughed, telling me the safety latch was secure so there was no danger. They kept prodding me – and for some stupid reason I pointed the gun at Irka. I knew the lock was secure so it seemed to be harmless. I went to pull the trigger in a mock act of shooting her and fortunately moved it just to the right at the last possible moment. The safety latch was not on, and the gun fired a loud pop. The bullet narrowly missed hitting her and went into the wall.

I was panic-stricken. Immediately I dropped the gun to the floor, dashed out of the house, and just kept running. I knew no one was injured, but I felt I had irreparably damaged my good standing with Mrs Lodzia. I was full of guilt and extremely angry with myself. After all Mrs Lodzia had done for me I had nearly killed her daughter. There was no way I could ever go back to her place again.

I walked around in circles all afternoon replaying my reckless behaviour over and over in my mind. Then evening approached and I wasn't sure what to do next. I was upset and I really needed a friend, so I went to visit Zybyszek.

Of everyone in our gang, he was my best friend. He was a couple of years older than me, so he was a little bigger than most of us. He had a powerful presence, exemplified by his sharply sarcastic sense of humour. He would make jokes about death and dying that would often seem inappropriate, but it was just his way of dealing with the insanity of our lives. He was also very tough. One time, a Polish youth came up and threatened us. He was a big boy – about eighteen or nineteen. 'You two are Jews aren't you?' he snapped at us. Whenever I heard the word Jew like that it felt as though a bullet was going through my heart. 'I want all your money and all your cigarettes,' he continued, 'or I'll give you away to the Germans.'

Zybyszek stood right up to the boy who was twice his size. 'You've got a nerve calling us Jews,' he fired back. 'We're not going to give you a single groszy. You just go ahead and call the Germans and we'll see what happens.' The boy tried to say something but Zybyszek wouldn't stop: 'You may be older than us, but you sure have a pea for a brain. Why are you threatening the two of us? Between us, we could beat your head in. And you know, maybe that's what we'll do.' Then he pulled out a knife he used for eating and pointed it at the boy.

That shmaltzer turned around and ran for his life. Zybyszek had extricated us from that predicament, but we still had to flee immediately and stay away from working in that neighbourhood for a long time. We couldn't take the chance that we might see him again, or perhaps he had run to get help from the Germans. I'll never know because we fortunately never came across him again.

Like me, Zybyszek had lost his entire family. He spoke fluent Polish, had shrewd business instincts and didn't look at all Jewish. In fact, he had blond hair and a round Aryan-like face. And he used those attributes fully in developing into quite a ladies' man. He would spread a blanket out at the market and sell cutlery on the ground. This brought him into contact with many young girls.

The day I almost shot Irka I arrived at his spot in the market as a nervous wreck. 'What's up Janek?' he asked casually. I told him about what happened and he couldn't believe his ears. His mood changed entirely. 'How could you do that?' he demanded. 'You've really screwed yourself.'

'I know, I know,' I told him. 'But there's nothing I can do about it now. What's done is done. The fact is that I'm back on the street again and I need a place to sleep. Where are you sleeping these days? Can I stay with you tonight?'

'Sure you can. I'm staying in the attics – rent-free. There's lots of room there, but no running water or toilets,' he joked, as his mood softened again.

I could have gone with the other cigarette sellers. Most of them stayed together in one place, but I hated it there. It was a house in which this crazy old lady rented rooms to drunks and other street people for ten zlotys a night.

Our friends' flat there was a pigsty. There was sooty dirt everywhere. Worse than that, the landlady had a mentally retarded daughter who kept animals such as rabbits – and they would be running around all over the place. I stayed there one time, and when I left I was so flea-bitten that I was red and itchy for two weeks. I vowed that I would never stay there again. To me, life on the streets was better than that disgusting place. I never could understand how my friends put up with it. Zybyszek was the only other one who hated it enough to avoid going there, though even if it had been a little nicer I don't think he would have stayed there because he preferred to be on his own. It wasn't that he didn't like the others, just that he was more comfortable as a loner.

Zybyszek had chosen an apartment building for us to sleep in. It was in an affluent area not far from where Mrs Lodzia lived. We arrived there just before curfew and went straight to the attic. I got settled into a potato bag I had brought with me and he laid down on a straw mat that he took with him wherever he went.

While we felt relatively safe and comfortable there was one problem. After curfew the front doors automatically locked. We were committed to staying there through the night. There was no way out if we ran into trouble.

We lay there quietly for a while – speaking in a soft whisper and not letting ourselves fall asleep so early that our snoring could give us away. Late into the night, when we felt confident that everyone else in the building had gone to bed we planned to have a short sleep.

About an hour after we settled in we heard footsteps and voices of two women getting nearer and nearer. Step by step they were climbing the stairs towards us. Before we could do anything, they unlocked the door and entered. Each was holding a basket of wet, washed clothes that were to be hung to dry in the attic.

They screamed when they saw us. 'Oh my God, what are you doing here. Are you Jews?' they asked. We maintained our poise, politely but firmly denying that we were Jewish. We explained that we were two farm boys who had come to the big city for a day of fun – and that we had so much of it that we lost track of time. 'Before long curfew was upon us and there was nothing we could do,' Zybyszek said. 'We didn't have enough money for a hotel room so this attic seemed to be the solution.'

'We'll be gone first thing in the morning because we've got to get back and take care of the cows,' I added.

The two women didn't believe us. 'You are Jews aren't you?' one of them insisted. 'You're hiding from the Germans and that's why you're here.' We vehemently denied it. 'We're as gentile as you are,' I protested. 'Do you want us to recite some prayers to prove it to you?'

'Do you really know prayers by heart?' she asked.

'Our father who art in heaven, hallowed be thy name ...'

'OK, OK,' she said before I could recite the rest of the prayer. 'I see that you could be Christians. So where are you boys from anyway?'

'We come from Wroclaw,' I said. 'My parents are dead and my grandmother looked after me from the time I was six years old. But she was very strict with me – too strict. She used to hit me whenever I didn't do exactly as she ordered. I couldn't wait until I was old enough to run away. I finally did and ended up at a farm about 30 kilometres from Warsaw working with the cows.'

Zybyszek then gave his story. He said that his father was an alcoholic who beat him constantly, and he couldn't take it any more so he ran away too. We both found work at the same farm which had posted a help-wanted sign.

'Poor boys,' the other woman said. 'You must be really hungry. After we hang our laundry we'll bring some food up for you.' We said that the offer was greatly appreciated and thanked them for their kindness. They quietly hung their laundry, smiled at us as they picked up their pails, and said they'd be back soon with some food. They locked the door on their way out.

We were very uneasy about the situation. At first they seemed convinced we were Jews. Then they said they believed our story and were going to give us food. It just didn't feel right, but there was nothing we could do. We were locked in; all we could do was hope the women believed our story.

Ten minutes later we again heard people coming up the stairs. This time the footsteps were heavier. The door opened and we saw two men. They looked intimidating – tall and muscular with rugged-looking faces.

'What are you doing here?' they demanded. 'Why are you sleeping on the floor like two drunks? Why did you pick this place? You told our wives you're from a farm but could not make it back in time. What's the real story?'

We rehashed the same explanation over and over again – insisting that every word we told their wives was true. We assured them that we were genuinely good boys who would not steal from them, and that we would be gone first thing in the morning. 'All right, we believe you,' the one man finally said. 'But you'd better be gone by 6 a.m. and you'd better leave this place as clean as when you arrived – no urinating.'

We promised to do as we were told, and thanked them for their kindness – telling them that God would reward them for their good deed. Their wives then handed each of us a sandwich.

'I hope we didn't get it wrong and we're actually feeding two Jew-boys,' the man said, with a cocky smirk on his face. 'Let's go,' he told the others, and they said goodnight to us while closing the door behind them.

We were worried that they had given us sandwiches laced with poison, but nothing was happening to either one of us. 'We're still alive, so I guess the food was safe,' Zybyszek said. 'That's a good sign.'

None the less, we knew we were still in big trouble. The way those men talked to us it was clear they didn't believe our story. We were worried sick that they were going to come back again. I was furious with myself. My life was in danger because of my bad behaviour. If only I had acted responsibly I'd have been safe in Mrs Lodzia's home.

A few hours later we heard footsteps climbing up the stairs. These did not sound the same as before. These were much heavier, louder, and there were more of them. We knew several people were coming for us, and we were terrified.

Then the door opened and I saw a flashlight in one hand and a gun in the other. There was a moment of eerie silence and then I heard a deep Polish voice say 'get up Jews'.

Our worst fears had been confirmed.

There were four men – two German gendarmes and two Polish policemen. All had their guns drawn and pointed at us. We were scared stiff, but fortunately, when they realized they were just dealing with two dirty little kids, they put their guns away.

'You're both Jews – rotten Jews, aren't you? Answer the question,' the one Polish policeman demanded. That man was particularly nasty.

'No, no, no!' we pleaded. 'We already told those married couples that we are gentile boys from the country.' After we repeated our story two or three times the hate-mongering Pole said he didn't believe a word of what we were saying. His reply was that if we really wanted to prove our identity we had to pull our pants down.

'If you're not circumcised, you're not Jewish, and we'll let you go,' the Pole said. 'On the other hand, if you are circumcised then we'll know you're Jewish and we'll deal with you accordingly.'

Rather than pull my pants all the way down, I just unzipped my fly, put my hand in, and pushed some skin over the top of my penis to make it look uncircumcised. He was wise to what I was doing so he yelled at me to pull my hand away.

112

At that moment one of the Germans moved forward. He had been standing quietly off to the side talking to the other German. He must have understood Polish because he seemed to be following exactly what was going on, translating what was being spoken into German for his colleague. I understood what he was saying because Yiddish – my native language – is very similar to German.

In German, the officer told the Polish policemen to leave and that he would take care of us himself. The cold-hearted Pole pleaded with him – insisting that we were Jewish. But the German pretended he didn't understand a word the Pole was saying and waved the two of them off.

Once they left, he turned to his German colleague and told him that we were not Jews, but that we were orphans just looking for a place to stay. For whatever reason, it seemed this Nazi was saving our lives – at least for the moment.

They took us down the stairs, out of the building and on to the street. We walked several blocks in the direction of a specific streetcar stand. By then it was just about morning, and we could hear passers-by callously yelling 'there are two Jews to be shot'.

We were cold, barefooted, lightly clothed, dirty and tired – and we did not know what was going on. Were we being taken to be shot? Were we going to a concentration camp? Were we actually being saved?

We arrived at the Kierbedria bridge stop and waited there. A streetcar No. 25 came by but we didn't take it. A few minutes later, a No. 26 arrived and we got on. We sat up at the front – the section for Germans only.

The No. 26 went through the Jewish cemetery so I figured we were being taken there to be shot, but before we got that far we disembarked at the Targowa Street stop – the site of the Gestapo headquarters building.

After going through the main entrance we went straight to

a commander's office. The Germans saluted their grey-haired boss with the 'Heil Hitler' sign, and the man saluted back. The commander asked if these were the two Jews in hiding. The German who brought us there replied that we were not Jews. He repeated our story, saying we were Polish orphans from Wroclaw, and he recommended that we be placed in an orphanage.

I could not believe it. This man really was doing his best to save our lives. As happy as I was, however, I couldn't show any emotion. We had to make them think we didn't understand what they were saying.

The commander signed a couple of papers and picked up the phone to make a quick call. A few moments later a guard came to pick us up. He took us to a jail cell and gave us some food. Several hours later a different man came to unlock us, asking which one of us was Janek and which was Zbigniew.

'You're on your way to an orphanage,' the officer said. 'And it's a really nice one with good food and schooling. You two are very lucky boys. There is a long waiting list to get into that place.'

It sounded like a dream! I wondered if maybe I really was dreaming.

As we left, the officer told us not to run away, and that we weren't going to be tied up. We walked beside him to a streetcar that took us to Leszna Street where the orphanage was located. He had papers in his hand, which had the stamp of approval from the Third Reich on the front page as well as a signature from the Gestapo Commandant.

He took us into the orphanage where he handed us and our papers to the priest who managed the place. It was home to about 30 boys aged eight to 15.

'So these are the two orphans,' the priest said. The officer confirmed it, wished us good luck and told us to behave ourselves or he'd be back for us. We assured him we would be very good boys.

What a break. In the morning, we figured we were dead. Now, we were in heaven – a clean, warm bed and ample food. And it was all because of that German. I'm sure he knew we were Jewish, but for some reason he had saved us.

The priest told us the nurse would give us a haircut – and then we'd be able to take a bath and change into some orphanage uniforms and clean socks. We came back to see him again once we were cleaned up.

He gave us a quick written test to assess our academic standing. He said I was at a Grade 4 level – and that I would start as a pupil in that grade. Then he told us our schedule. Each day we would be up at 6 a.m. for a shower. Then we would go to the chapel for prayers before eating breakfast. From 8 a.m. until noon we would have classes. Lunch would be until 1 p.m., after which we would return to class until 3.30 p.m. We would have time to play games and do our homework until 5.30 p.m. Then we'd have supper, go to chapel for more prayers at 7.30 p.m. and be in our beds by 8 p.m. Lights were to be out by 8.30 p.m.

'Is that understood?' he asked.

'That sounds just fine,' we said.

When suppertime came that night, we were introduced to all the other orphans. We sat at a table with regular forks and knives and napkins. The food was delicious, though it was a little strange to have to thank Jesus before and after the meal.

I got along very well with the priest, and I think he took a liking to me right from the start. Within my first couple of days in the orphanage he asked if we had taken first communion. Being three years older than me Zybyszek said he had. I told the priest I had not, and he saw that as a wonderful opportunity. He relished the chance to prepare me for the big occasion. He got me singing in the choir, and gave me postcards with pictures of Jesus on them – which I hung over my bed like a good Catholic boy.

After about a week of preparation I went to first communion. I felt extremely odd. It was one thing to masquerade as a non-Jew, but quite another to take the communion. Despite the discomfort of having Catholicism shoved down my throat, it was heaven on earth there, masking what was happening in the outside world; it didn't even seem as if a war was going on.

Then, less than two weeks later, it all came to a sudden and abrupt end.

At the daily showers, we were inspected by the orphanage nurse to see if we had washed well enough and whether or not we had infections or wounds she should be aware of. Each time Zybyszek and I took a shower we managed to slip past her, but finally one morning she called me over.

'Janek, why are you always avoiding me?' she asked. 'Is there some kind of problem?'

'No, there is no problem,' I replied. 'I am just shy and not comfortable having a woman look at my nude body. That's all. Besides, I'm not a two year-old. I'm perfectly capable of washing myself. Don't you think so?'

'No, not at all,' she said sternly. 'I am the nurse and I see who I want when I want. Do you understand?'

'Yes,' I said. This woman was tough as nails. It was unwise to aggravate her. She told me to hold my hands up and proceeded to examine me thoroughly. 'Now I know why you were avoiding me,' she exclaimed. 'You are a Jew and you don't belong here. I can see it right here. You are circumcised.'

'I am not a Jew,' I retorted. 'What do you mean by circumcised?' She said circumcision was what separated Jews from gentiles – that on the eighth day of life Jewish boys had their foreskins removed.

'Oh that,' I said. 'Well, when I was little I fell on a nail and I had to go to the doctor and have it fixed. He did a good job

116

on it don't you think?' She looked a little confused by my reply, didn't comment on it, and told me to get dressed.

About 15 minutes later I heard an announcement over the loudspeaker: 'Janek Jankowski, please come down to the doctor's office immediately.'

I had a sinking feeling in my stomach that I was in major trouble. If only that nurse had some human feeling, she could easily have just forgotten the whole thing, but because of her I was terrified, unsure about what to do.

Over the next few minutes, as my name was repeated two more times, I searched for and found Zybyszek. I told him what had happened and asked him what he thought I should do. He said to go up to the doctor's office, hear what she had to say and then decide what to do. I agreed that seemed to be the most prudent approach, so I reluctantly went up to the doctor's office. I was taken in right away.

There was a female doctor sitting at her desk. Like the nurse, she was all business and got straight to the point: 'Janek, Nurse Basia just told me that after examining you in the shower, she has come to the conclusion that you have been circumcised and that you are Jewish. Drop your pants down and let me have a look. I will be the final judge in this matter.'

I did as she ordered and she carefully inspected me in silence. After a few moments that seemed to take ages she finally said, 'Nurse Basia was absolutely correct. You are a Jewish boy.'

I expected her to come to that conclusion, and had given some thought on how to counter her accusation. I described my story about the nail again, and added another line of argument to bolster my defence. 'Doctor, you are a smart woman. If I am Jewish why would I have arrived here hand-delivered by the Germans with all the necessary documents? If I was a Jew, they would have shot me.'

'That may be so,' she said. 'Nevertheless, you have been

circumcised and therefore you are a Jew. As to what happened to get you here, I will look into it.'

I tried one last time. 'Look doctor, is it not possible that falling on a nail would require an operation that would result in a different-looking penis?'

'Yes, that is true. But you are cleanly circumcised. There was no accident.' That was the end of the argument.

'Now go and get changed and play with the others,' she said. 'I will look into this and get back to you later.'

I got my stuff together and dashed down the stairs. Zybyszek was on tenterhooks waiting for me. 'What happened up there? What did she say? Tell me, are we in trouble?' he asked, realizing that they'd soon call him to the office and see that he too was circumcised.

'We're in trouble,' I replied. 'She didn't believe a word of the story I gave her. I think the only thing to do now is get out of here before the police show up and arrest us. This time we won't be so lucky. She's probably calling them right now.'

Moments later we jumped through the gate in our light uniforms and ran off as fast as we could. We searched through various places in a nearby neighbourhood where laundry was hanging and eventually found some shirts and pants that fitted us.

After a while, daylight started to fade and we were getting really hungry. Unfortunately, we had no money. We made it to a small store just before closing time, where we asked if they had any bread they could spare for two poor children. They were just about to throw out some day-old bread and gave it to us instead. We were very grateful.

Soon after, we stumbled upon a nearby park and decided to stay there. We were so tired we fell asleep quite quickly. We just hoped we wouldn't be caught as had happened a couple of weeks earlier. What a turnaround we had experienced in a matter of just a few hours. We had thought we were safe with a warm bed to sleep in and good cooked meals, and all of a sudden we were back where we began. I was thinking about what awful people the nurse and the doctor were. Their professions were to help people, but all they wanted to do was get us killed. On the bright side, however, at least we were free and alive. We had a peaceful night of sleep as it was unusually warm for autumn.

The next morning we decided to split up. Zybyszek had a few places to turn to – and ended up back in business in the market. A few weeks later, he was taken in by a local family.

I, on the other hand, realized there was only one thing I could do. I had to go back to Mrs Lodzia's and hope she would forgive me. I decided that at the very least I owed it to her to let her know how sorry I was for what I had done. I jumped on to the tail of a streetcar going to Saska Kepa and was on my way.

When I got to her doorstep, my heart was pounding like crazy. I knocked and she opened the door. 'Oh my God,' she said. 'I'm so happy to see you. We were sure you were dead!' She was so excited to see me. She hugged me and brought me inside. 'Where have you been for the past two weeks? How could you not let us know where you were? That was not fair of you Janek.'

'Let me explain,' I interrupted. 'Let me tell you everything and then you'll understand that it wasn't my fault.'

I told her about the boys and the gun and apologized for my actions. She said Irka told her all about it and that it was old news. She was more interested in what happened to me since then. She was shocked when she heard about my adventure. As I was finishing my story, she told me she wanted to make me something to eat and invited me to continue staying at her place.

I said that was very gracious, but that I would only do it if the girls still wanted me there. When they came home from school and saw me they reacted just as their mother had –

they jumped all over me with enthusiasm. They called me a cat with nine lives after I told them about my past two weeks, but I'm not sure that's true. After all I had been through between 1939 and the end of 1943, I think I escaped the clutches of death many more than nine times.

Fortunately, with the Germans losing ground to the Soviets day by day, 1944 looked as if it would be a better year for me. But there was still a way to go yet before my Nazi nightmare would end.

8 · Liberation

Had it not been for the war, I would have been preparing for my bar mitzvah during the first few months of 1944. But that was a distant dream. Life on the street was the only reality I knew.

While surviving was not easy, I had grown more and more accustomed to my circumstances, and found street life at the later stages in the war to be much more manageable than the earlier days of smuggling myself into and out of the ghetto. In Three Crosses Square, I had fake identity papers, including a special pass to ride the streetcars, which I used often for the commute between 'work' selling cigarettes and my 'home' with Mrs Lodzia in Saska Kepa.

Week by week, I became better and better at selling and began to take in more money. One of the secrets of my business success was a tall blonde woman I met in the Three Crosses area. She worked in a nightclub that provided entertainment for the Germans. I think she was a prostitute. Her clients would pay her with cigarettes – far more than she would ever need. Whenever this happened, which was at least once or twice a week, she would walk past me carrying a particular handbag, which was her signal to me that I was to go to her apartment building. She would let me up to her flat where I would purchase the high-quality cigarettes from her. I bought them at dirt-cheap prices and then sold them for a handsome profit.

While that kind of business success led to a strong confidence that I had a good chance of surviving the war, life was still extremely dangerous. The fate of a couple of my cigarette-selling buddies reminded me of this.

One boy who we called 'Kulas', which roughly translated

means someone who limps, was turned in by some schmaltzers and taken away to the Gestapo headquarters. We never saw him again. He was probably shot.

Then there was the sad end of another boy we called Frenchy. His family was from France, but of Polish origin, and was deported to Warsaw after France fell to Germany. Frenchy, who looked very Parisian, was the last remaining member of his family. Before the war, his parents had befriended a German official who lived in Paris. One day Frenchy saw that same man near Three Crosses Square. The officer presented himself as a long-lost 'friend' and invited Frenchy to his place for a visit. When Frenchy got there, the man took him to the Gestapo headquarters. The boy was never seen or heard of again.

While those were the worst of times in 1944, there were some great moments too. The best of all came on 22 April when I celebrated my 13th birthday. Remembering how awful my 12th was, I was determined to have a good time, and I can thank Mrs Lodzia for making it happen.

My idea was to have a birthday party – something I hadn't experienced since I was eight years old. I didn't want to have it at our apartment because that was too dangerous, but all my friends were nagging at me to ask Mrs Lodzia anyway. They realized that no one else could be approached about such a thing and they were more desperate for a party than even I was. Somehow, they talked me into asking her.

To my surprise she agreed to the idea but set some conditions for it. All my friends had to arrive one at a time at 10-minute intervals and leave the same way. And everyone had to keep relatively quiet so as not to arouse any suspicion.

While Mrs Lodzia made cabbage rolls and sauerkraut, each of the gang brought something with them – vodka, sausages, buns and fruits. Someone even brought a cake.

After Irving started the evening with some prayers, we

proceeded to have a wonderful time. I expended so much energy I was exhausted (and a little drunk) and fell asleep before the end of the evening. The boys played a trick on me by placing hard-boiled eggs under my bottom – which gave me quite a surprise when I awoke.

The next morning everyone left – the same way they had arrived – one by one, 10 minutes apart. For all of us, the party was a night to remember for the rest of our lives – and it was all possible because Mrs Lodzia had such a big heart.

I remember one other time that spring when Mrs Lodzia took a major risk to help our friend Stasiek – the one we called 'Golec'. He was about 18 years old and was the most difficult rebel of the group – even worse than Zybyszek. But he had a valuable role to play. He was a real tough guy who could keep the shmaltzers away.

As the war effort looked less promising, the Germans began rounding up Poles to take back to Germany so they could have additional labour for their factories. I was safe from this because I looked so young. Golec, however, appeared to be in his twenties, and was picked up one day in Three Crosses Square. We thought we would never see him again – that the Germans would interrogate him and ultimately discover his identity and shoot him. But the idea that he might be Jewish didn't occur to them. They were anxious for labour and figured he was Polish, so they shaved his head and hastily sent him away to work. Somehow, Golec escaped and came back to Warsaw. However, with his shaven head he could easily have been spotted and identified by the Germans and then he'd have been in big trouble.

He desperately needed a place to hide, and when I told Mrs Lodzia about his predicament she suggested I bring him to her place and she would hide him for a few days. He ended up staying with us for a week. We got him a toupée and a fake moustache so that not even his mother would have recognized him. When he re-emerged, he protected himself by leaving Saska Kepa and working the streets of another district.

By the late spring and early summer of 1944 Germany did more than just take young men away for labour. More Germans were being brought into Warsaw, they were making themselves more visible, and they became much more oppressive towards all Poles, who were increasingly gaining confidence as the Russians drew closer on the Eastern Front. Under the tougher conditions I was very lucky to have had the safe haven of Mrs Lodzia's because it would have been more difficult than ever to be sleeping in parks and attics. The only advantage to the increased number of Germans was the opportunity to make some extra money. As the war turned more sharply against Hitler, newspapers became increasingly popular, and I spent more time profitably selling them than I did selling cigarettes.

On 1 August 1944, Russian advance patrols neared the eastern suburbs of Warsaw. In fact, from Mrs Lodzia's neighbourhood we could hear some shelling off in the distance. It was difficult to contain our excitement thinking that any day we could be liberated. The Poles certainly felt this way. Confident that they would receive help from the Russians, a spirited Polish uprising was launched to take the city back from the Germans. The Poles enjoyed some early success, quickly gaining control over most of central Warsaw.

But this masked a serious problem. The Polish resistance was being led by the 'Armia Krajowa', whose orders came from the British-backed Polish Government in London. People in the Armia Krajowa were as anti-Soviet as they were anti-German. Not surprisingly, the Russians didn't support this army and were furious with the Polish populace for embracing them.

Because of this, the Russians decided to slow their progress

124

and let the Poles and the Germans kill each other in Warsaw. Churchill wasn't happy with this but couldn't get Stalin to change his mind. Britain tried some independent airdrops to help the Poles but most of the supplies fell into German hands.

Once the Germans moved reinforcements into Warsaw, and realized that the Poles were on their own, they recaptured the momentum and mercilessly pounded the city. I was lucky to be in Saska Kepa, which was on the eastern edge of the Vistula. The German–Polish battle was restricted to everywhere west of the Vistula. The bridge back into the city had been bombed so while we found ourselves literally metres from the war zone, our suburb was safe with the Russians quietly waiting off to the east of us.

The main problem for us was food becoming scarce and much more expensive. The situation prompted me to go on a little adventure one day in late August of 1944. My two crazy Catholic friends who shot the German told me that in Malkinia, which was about 50 miles to the east (near Treblinka), lard could be exchanged for cigarettes. I knew we needed a lot of lard at home, and any excess would be in such great demand that I could sell the rest and make enough money to buy a good amount of other essentials.

I asked Mrs Lodzia what she thought of my idea and she just shrugged her shoulders. She said that I was my own boss who could decide for myself what to do. I agreed, so without much hesitation I chose to go. I reasoned that it would only be for four days, it could be a fun adventure, and most important of all, I could really help Mrs Lodzia and her daughters if the trip was successful.

We left that day, jumping on a cattle train for the journey. I felt very sad on that trip. The trains were the same ones that were previously used to transport Jews to Treblinka – including my brother and my sister. I felt awful the whole way there, but once we got to our destination I was able to put those horrible thoughts behind me and focus on the job in hand.

After sleeping outdoors for the night, we acquired the lard early the next day. With 15 kilos of the stuff for each of us to take back to Saska Kepa, we anxiously went to catch a train home. However, when we arrived at the station we found that the trains weren't running because the Russians were nearing Malkinia. This created a big problem for us.

The weather was really hot, and we were afraid that if we had to wait too long the lard would go rancid, so we made a fast decision to return on foot. Without wasting another minute, we starting walking towards Warsaw and I quickly realized that I was in for an extremely difficult journey. Unlike the other two stronger, older boys I was very small for a boy of 13, so it was a real struggle in the heat and humidity with all that lard on my back. We must have covered about half the distance on the first day before mercifully we slept in a field for the night.

We got up early the next morning hoping that we could finish the journey by nightfall. But the advancing Russian army was quickly catching up to us. We could hear artillery explosions and see planes flying overhead. We had to run for cover when they got really close, and a farmer took us in just before the shelling intensified. We emerged when the explosions stopped and saw the Russian army in the nearby village. I felt absolutely euphoric. How I had longed to see the day the Germans would be defeated. I kept telling myself I was finally free.

Unfortunately, I was a little premature in that assessment.

The enemy came back with a blistering counter-offensive and six hours later the territory was back in German hands. I didn't know it at the time, but the reason the Germans regained the land wasn't just because of their firepower. The Russians had pulled back voluntarily, as a result of their displeasure with the Polish uprising in Warsaw.

After the fighting subsided we resumed our trek to Saska Kepa. We had to pass through German lines which was quite scary because they were dug into positions and had their machine guns pointed at us as we walked down the street. We were fortunate they let us go by without incident.

Several hours later, I made it back to Mrs Lodzia's apartment. She was extremely relieved to see me back in one piece. 'I was so worried about you,' she said. 'We heard the Russian army was advancing and that the trains had stopped running. I wasn't sure you'd be able to make it back.'

'Nothing is going to happen to me,' I reassured her. 'I feel quite fine. And how are the girls?' I asked, demonstrating that confidence by casually changing the subject. 'Worried sick like me,' she replied.

Shortly after, the mood changed for the better as everyone realized that despite my difficult ordeal I did accomplish my mission. I had brought back all the lard. Mrs Lodzia kept a large portion of it and I sold the rest. The excursion was worth it after all.

In the meantime, the Poles were being hammered by the Germans in Warsaw, with the battle raging for about two months. The Poles fought with Molotov cocktails, light machine guns and mortars. The Germans had heavy artillery at their disposal, and the manpower to go house-to-house and room-to-room in order to weed out the resistance. It was the closest the Poles ever came to knowing what it felt like for the Jews.

By the time the uprising ended, the Poles had killed some 10,000–20,000 Germans. Meanwhile, as many as 250,000 Poles were dead, and about 20,000–40,000 Armia Krajowa fighters were captured and taken to Germany. My two friends Pavel and Zenek were in Warsaw during this time. While hiding their Jewish identity, they fought with the Armia Krajowa against the Germans. They were among those taken away to Germany.

With the Poles destroyed and the Germans weakened and in retreat, the Soviets were ready to begin moving in. As they prepared to resume their push, we waited patiently for liberation in Saska Kepa.

When the Soviets did make their move, we could see how the momentum was clearly in their favour. Each day, there were more and more Soviet planes in the air and fewer and fewer German ones. Sometimes you could watch the battles in the air – and the Germans were losing almost every single one of them.

The Germans were getting licked and it was only a matter of time until we would be free. I was very excited but the Poles weren't. They hated the Russians for conquering Poland in partnership with the Germans. I couldn't have cared less. I would much rather have been occupied by the Soviets than the Nazis.

Liberation day finally arrived in the spring of 1945. It was somewhat anti-climactic because it seemed to take the Soviets for ever when they could have come so much sooner, but it felt wonderful none the less. I was no longer a hunted animal.

After the initial joy, however, my feelings began to change. I had lived to see the last day of the war, and the reality of my tragedy started to sink in. Life for the past six years had consisted of nothing more than existing hour-to-hour and day-to-day, just fighting for survival. There was no time and no reason to consider the future. But with liberation I had to think about what to do with the rest of my life. My family was all gone and I had neither wealth nor education as a foundation. The war had taken everything away from me. It was depressing and frustrating.

Fortunately, I also realized that I was lucky to be alive and that – as I told myself many times during the war – life is to be cherished and each moment seized. I had fought so long and hard for survival that I couldn't let it go to waste. I was determined to build a new life for myself. While I loved Mrs Lodzia and her family very much, I decided it was best to leave Poland and start afresh. Warsaw had brought me nothing but heartache and sorrow, and I knew my best chance of happiness would be far away from it.

I still wanted to stay for a while, hoping that I could make contact with some relatives who had survived. I thought they might be looking for me just as I was looking for them and that we'd connect. I especially wanted to investigate my brother Getzel's fate. After fleeing to Russia, I thought he had perhaps joined the army and was alive somewhere in the Soviet Union or even in Poland. I wrote to his old address and to the Moscow Red Cross, but I received no response.

Meanwhile, Mrs Lodzia continued to give me her unconditional support, and told me I could stay with her as long as I wanted and was free to leave whenever I wanted.

My next move came shortly after liberation when a Polish boy I knew introduced me to a few Jewish soldiers from Russia. The boy had served in the 'Armia Ludowa'. During the uprising against the Germans, not all the Poles had fought with the Armia Krajowa. There was also the Armia Ludowa, which was allied to the Soviets instead of to the London Poles and the British. This group of soldiers mixed with the Soviets, who had a number of Jews amongst them looking for Jewish survivors.

I was greeted somewhat reluctantly by the soldiers. At first they did not believe me when I told them I was Jewish. They asked all kinds of questions about Judaism and my answers only partially convinced them. They asked if I could speak Yiddish and I told them I could, but after three years of only Polish on the Aryan side it wasn't so easy. My brain and mouth weren't cooperating; my mind was willing and able to converse, but my mouth had other ideas. I paused for a few moments to calm down and concentrate, and over the next few minutes it all started to flow. It felt wonderful to be speaking my native language again, and that was what finally convinced them I was Jewish.

When I told them my goal was to get out of Poland, the leader of the group said I should go to Lublin, about 100 miles south-east of Warsaw.

'The sooner you get there, the sooner you'll leave the country,' he said.

I decided to leave. I had experienced a few weeks of unsuccessful searching in which I couldn't find a single surviving family member in Warsaw, so there was no reason to stay there any longer. My thinking was that I could resume my search in Lublin for a while, and if I still couldn't find anyone by the time I had an opportunity to leave the country, so be it.

I went to get my things together, which didn't take long. All I had were three cameras (I'm still not sure why I had three), a few toiletries, some clothes, several silver pieces and a rucksack to put everything in. Then came the hard part – saying goodbye to Mrs Lodzia and her two daughters. I hugged and kissed the woman to whom I owe my life today. I promised her and her daughters that I would never forget them and that I would always remain in touch. With tears in my eyes I headed off.

Now that I was ready to leave there was still one problem. Transportation was hard to come by because the trains weren't running. The railways were demolished from the battles between the Germans and the Soviets so I had to ask around and finally arrived at a solution. I discovered a group of Russian soldiers who were going to Lublin in a flatbed military truck. They offered to let me come along.

It was quite risky for me to go with them because had they opened my bag they would have discovered that I had three cameras in it and they could have thought I was a spy. That would have resulted in getting tossed off the truck or being shot. Lucky for me they never saw what was in the bag so I was fine.

When I arrived in Lublin I headed straight to the marketplace. The goal was to sell all my stuff so I'd have enough money for food and lodging. I didn't know what to ask as a selling price for my cameras so I started at a high price and worked my way down until I got some takers. The clothes were easy to sell, and by the end of the day I had a good sum of zlotys in my pocket.

I then went to a part of town where – according to the Jewish soldiers – some surviving Jews from around Poland had congregated. I entered a restaurant in that area – starving and looking forward to a special meal. I sat down and a waiter came over to serve me. He looked very unimpressed and treated me like dirt. But I wasn't about to let him bother me. I ordered a large portion of Jewish-style roasted chicken. It was one of the most expensive items on the menu and he asked me if I had enough money to pay for it. His eyes popped out when I took out one of the three bundles of money which I had acquired from my sales in the marketplace. After that, he started treating me more like a real customer. I thought to myself: 'If he thinks he's getting a good tip out of this he's got a surprise waiting for him.'

The restaurant had an accordion player for the entertainment of all the patrons. His name was Ludwig – Lutek in Polish. He was a deserter from the Soviet army who played music for a living. When he came to my table to see if I had any requests, I took out a few zlotys and asked him if he knew the song 'Treblinka'. It was a sad song that had been written about that death camp and had become somewhat of an anthem for the Jews of Warsaw. He said he knew the song and began to play it.

I started to sing along and then everyone in the restaurant turned their heads towards my table and listened intently to our rendition. Some people started to cry openly. When the song ended, Lutek complimented me on my singing voice and asked me if I wanted to work with him in the restaurant that night. I finished my meal and joined him. We had a great time and he was quite pleased with me.

At the end of the night, he asked if I wanted to work with him on a regular basis. He explained that the restaurant was only one of several venues he played at. He also did weddings – both Jewish and Polish – and various other private parties.

My plan was to use my remaining zlotys and go into business for myself in the marketplace. Then, after acquiring more money, I expected to travel to a few more towns in search of relatives. I wasn't sure whether working in the marketplace or singing with Lutek would pay more, so I told him I would think carefully about his offer and let him know in a few days.

He wouldn't accept this, however, and became very persistent that I join him. After several minutes of his harassment, I finally I agreed to work with him – but only after I took one last trip. The trains were running again and I went to Lodz for several days to register my name for surviving family members and to buy some silk clothes that I knew were available there and in demand in Lublin.

Over the next few days I came to realize the Russian who told me Lublin was the route to getting out of Poland was mistaken. Any possibility of leaving was still a long time away, so when I came back from Lodz I decided to settle in Lublin for a while until the right opportunity to flee the country presented itself. That was frustrating, but at least I had a little more time to see if any relatives would surface.

When I returned from Lodz, Lutek had a new job playing his

accordion in a mobile military hospital. He asked me to join a band he had quickly put together. His group consisted of four other wounded soldiers who played the violin, trumpet, guitar and saxophone. They needed a drummer – and Lutek asked me if I would take on that role. The idea of playing in a band sounded fun so I abandoned my silk-selling ideas and joined his group. I got my hands on a set of drums and I was all set to go. They even made a uniform for me. I looked just like a Polish soldier – boots and all.

I was the centre of attention wherever we would play – the pet of the group who was just a small young boy playing in a band with adults. For the most part, it was a lot of fun. I was also given the chance to sing, which I later regretted because I think it ruined my vocal chords. (I was going through puberty at the time and my voice was breaking.)

One day, not long after starting to work with them, I came down with a bad cold. I think it had to do with my return trip from Lodz when I had to stay on the roof of a train in the pouring rain. Within a couple of days my cold got much worse and before I knew it I was in a hospital bed suffering from pneumonia. In those days they didn't have antibiotics so I had to get by essentially untreated. At least the hospital was very good to me. I was even placed in a room that was designated for officers. Eventually I pulled through, but it took me weeks to recover fully.

During my illness our hospital was ordered to get closer to the new front lines. As 1945 progressed, the Russians were moving further into German territory, and the hospital was moved to the Gulf of Danzig, placed in a pretty, popular town called Sopot.

After I was fully recovered from my illness, our band got a job playing in a Sopot nightclub, from 9 p.m. to 4 a.m. This was on top of our regular jobs playing for the wounded soldiers in the hospital, so we were making some decent money – but working really hard.

I got hold of a new, better set of drums and really started to have fun with them as I became more comfortable with my role. Some of those nights were crazy. For example, people loved it and would buy drinks of vodka for each of us in the band whenever we played the song 'Warsrawa'. At first I drank the booze, but after a while I realized it wasn't doing me any good and I asked the nightclub owner to bring me water instead.

Even though I was having lots of fun there, there were some depressing realities that kept me from true happiness. First, I was not free to be a Jew. I never gave away my Jewish identity – and neither did Lutek. Anti-Semitism was still rampant, and after the war pogroms victimizing the few remaining survivors were common throughout Poland. I also found out later that the much-respected head of the Sopot hospital was Jewish. She was a colonel in the Polish army who hid her Jewishness too. Neither Lutek nor I knew her real identity.

The anti-Semitism reminded me of the true reason I was staying there. It wasn't to play songs. It was to find relatives who might still be alive, and then to leave Poland. In time it became clear that I wasn't going to find any family members, so it was time to leave.

My goal was to be with other stranded Jews like me. I wanted to go to Palestine, to help build Israel – the Jewish nation. Unfortunately, that was easier said than done in 1945. The British weren't letting Jews in – and many who tried found themselves in detention camps in Cyprus. I didn't want to end up there so I decided that it would be best to get to England or America and then go to Israel later. But first I had to get out of Poland, where any dreams of the future were destined to be quashed by the nightmares of my past.

The initial promise that Lublin was a quick route out of Poland had been a setback. But eventually Lutek found out about an opportunity that seemed quite promising. Over time, he too decided it was best to leave Poland, and through his network had learned that if we could get to Krakow, we could pick up false papers that would gain us entry into Germany.

We got there as quickly as possible, and found out that it was true – for a small fee we could have papers made up saying that we were French. The plan was to get on a train that would take us to Czechoslovakia, at which point we would switch to another train that would take us into Germany. It was unclear where I would go from there – but it would be to a safe haven outside Germany. It sounded great, but I wasn't about to get too excited until it actually materialized.

We boarded our train with our meagre belongings and set off towards Prague. Lutek spoke French so he told me that if we got into any trouble, all I had to say was 'oui, oui'. He would handle the rest. At the border, they came to check our papers. When Lutek asked me in French to hand mine to him so he could give both to the border agent, I said, as instructed, 'oui, oui'. The man looked at our documents for a second and moved on. The hurdle was cleared.

We changed trains and before we knew it we were in German territory. We disembarked in the city of Straubing in Bavaria. The Americans were occupying that territory, so we walked to one of their main compounds. Lutek had been instructed to go and see a certain major in the US military who was Jewish. The man was waiting for us.

The major told me I would be flown from Germany to England – where I would be placed in a Jewish orphanage. I was so excited I wanted to scream. In a matter of hours, I'd be on my way to a whole new life.

9 • After the War

To get to Britain, we flew in a plane that was carrying American parachutists. It was such a dramatic way to travel. I was so excited just being on an aeroplane – let alone a military plane which had been used to help defeat the Nazis.

I was coming to England thanks to the Jewish Congress of England, which sponsored the transport of some one thousand orphaned children to London. Along with 23 other survivors, I was placed in a hostel in the city of Northampton.

The head was a 65-year-old German Jew, assisted by his 40-year-old daughter Esther. They worked extremely hard to help us from the moment we arrived. I was very small and short due to a lack of proper nourishment during the war, so they put me on a special nutritional programme to boost my growth. This worked as I grew several inches between the ages of 14 and 16, though only to a final height of about five foot, two inches.

We were well cared for in all respects, including being sent to a nearby school. Unfortunately, I was not among the best behaved of children. In fact, I'm sure I was quite a pain in the neck for the head and his daughter. I remember that Queenie, their beautiful, three-year-old dog had never been spayed. Esther didn't take her eyes off the dog when it was on heat, making sure Queenie wouldn't run away in search of a male companion. I kept telling Esther she was a cruel person by making the animal suffer so much. I told her she should either allow Queenie to get pregnant or spay her, so that the poor dog wouldn't be looking for a mate all the time. But Esther refused to listen no matter how often I said it.

So one evening when Esther was out for dinner I brought a hideous-looking male dog into the hostel and let it loose on

136

Queenie. A few weeks later, Queenie gave birth to six of the most unsightly puppies imaginable. Esther was livid and tried to find out who was responsible, but no one said anything so I was never punished. She gave the puppies away and finally took Queenie to be spayed.

I was also a handful for her father, who was a devoutly religious man. I had been raised in a strict Orthodox Jewish family, but that life was a distant memory. At the hostel, I totally rejected anything to do with Judaism. Whenever he put a *yarmulke* on my head, I threw it to the floor. When the time came to say prayers, I refused to take part. I could not worship a God I did not believe existed.

'How could a God have sentenced one million innocent children to death in gas chambers?' I would ask indignantly. 'How could he allow demented Germans to derive pleasure from their slaughter? If Almighty God was so wonderful and powerful, why didn't he stop the Germans before they nearly wiped out an entire race of people?'

I told the head the sooner he accepted the fact that I would not participate in his prayer sessions, the better we would get along. At one point, I even asked to be sent to another hostel where religion wasn't practised. The man refused to give up on me, however, telling me God worked in mysterious ways and everything had happened to me for a reason. He told me that one day I would change my thinking. After I had a family of my own and did well in the world, he said, I would thank God for the gift of life.

The head was a father figure to me – a kindly man who had an uncanny ability to connect with children. No matter how angry I became, I could never hold it against him. Eventually, after talking to me daily for many months, he convinced me that my rejection of religion was just a way of venting all my anger and frustration. I did feel fortunate to be alive with a chance at a prosperous future, and I began to accept his belief that I had God to thank for it. This more positive attitude improved my outlook on everything, especially schooling. I had been at school for only two years in Warsaw before the war came along, so I had an enormous challenge to catch up with everyone else. I set about my studies with vigorous energy, determined to make up for lost time. In six months I blazed through the equivalent of eight years of school.

After that, I went on to a trade school to specialize in tool and die-making, where we spent half our time learning how to use the machinery, and the other half studying English, maths and other academic subjects. Within two years, I completed the course-work for my diploma.

In addition to my studies, the headmaster insisted I play the violin, letting me use the same instrument that he played when he was a boy. I took lessons and learned a great deal, even though I wasn't too enthusiastic about it because I would have preferred to play another instrument, such as the saxophone.

My lessons were paid for by a Mr Rothschild, who often came to the hostel to hear what his money had produced. Each time, I would spend hours practising the pieces I had learned so I wouldn't embarrass myself. I wasn't a star but I did all right; I was good enough to play 'Ava Maria' in the third and fourth positions. I recall that the moment Mr Rothschild left, I immediately packed the violin away and returned to the soccer field to enjoy my great passion.

Towards the end of my schooling, I was transferred to a new hostel in London. I preferred it there because I could play soccer in a citywide junior league, participate in a youth club, and continue to study tool and die-making. All my friends in Northampton were jealous that I was able to live in the big city, especially because I could now see all the top professional soccer teams.

The head at the new hostel tried to expose us to as much culture as possible, and took us on a tour of London one time on a very cold and wet day. We toured museums and other sights but I didn't enjoy it much because I had a sore throat. Over the next few days I felt worse so a doctor examined me. He diagnosed diphtheria, and had me immediately rushed to the hospital and put in the isolation ward. There I was treated with a new wonder drug called penicillin. Over the next few weeks I slowly recovered.

Not long after that I suffered an appendicitis attack. The doctor wanted to operate on me, but also told me there was a chance I could get better without an operation because the appendix was not inflamed to a crisis point. He cautioned that at some point in the future, however, surgery would be necessary because the next attack would be much more serious.

I reasoned that people die on the operating table, and even if it were to go smoothly it would hardly be a pleasant experience. I recalled how a friend recently had to spend two weeks in bed recuperating from an appendix operation. I felt there was no emergency yet, and if I reduced my swimming and diving I wouldn't aggravate the appendix, and could prevent another attack. I think the experience of surviving the war gave me a false sense of invincibility; I actually believed that because I made it through the Holocaust, I could beat the appendicitis without an operation. As a result, I decided to put off having an operation for as long as possible, if not altogether. In the short term at least, my gamble paid off as the appendix problem soon faded away.

Once I recovered, I was happier than ever in the new orphanage. London was fascinating, and life was full of fun with my soccer and other interests such as going to Hyde Park on Sunday afternoons to listen to people exercising their freedom of speech. It had been just a matter of months since I was struggling to survive under a cruel Nazi regime, and here I was a completely free young man who had his life in front of him. But there still was that emptiness, that sadness in my heart which I would be forced to endure for the rest of my life. Having lost everyone, there was no one with whom I could share my exciting new life.

By the end of 1947 I was finished with all my schooling and training and was ready to go to Palestine to pursue a career as a tradesman. The official creation of Israel was just around the corner. I now just had to be patient for a little longer until Jews would be able to immigrate there legally.

However, patience was never one of my strengths. One day in January 1948 I heard that the Canadian Jewish Congress was bringing to Canada 100 children who survived the Holocaust. Some were to come from orphanages in England, so I applied, thinking I had nothing to lose and it might be a fun move. There was nothing forcing me to stay in Canada if I didn't like it there so I figured I should take advantage of the opportunity to see another country in a different part of the world. I felt I could still move to Israel after experiencing Canada for a while.

I applied one morning in January 1948, and only 10 days later I was on my way. All I had to do was to pass a medical exam and have a brief interview with Canadian government officials.

Like the other orphans going on the trip, I was really excited to be going across the Atlantic on the *Aquitania* – a massive oceanliner. As it departed from Southampton on 4 February 1948, all I had was $40 in Canadian currency, a bag full of clothes, an accordion, a violin the Northampton head gave me as a going-away gift, a few school books, and some photos and other memorabilia from two and a half wonderful years in England.

Excited to be embarking on such a great adventure, I was sitting at the piano playing tunes, singing songs and drinking beer only moments after hitting the high seas. But the fun lasted all of about one hour. It took four days to get to Halifax and I was sick on each of them. With the exception of that first hour, I spent the whole trip in bed.

On the fifth day, a Friday afternoon, we arrived in Halifax where we were greeted by members of the city's Jewish community and a reporter from the local newspaper. (The headline of the article, which I still have, read: 'Survivors of the Holocaust – Jewish orphans arrive in Canada'.) We spent the weekend in Halifax before heading on to Montreal and Toronto.

Each of us was placed in a Jewish home for our two days on the East Coast. I stayed with the Zaife family. Mr Zaife, the president of the local Jewish congregation, owned a large furniture store. He, his wife and only daughter lived in an elegant, huge home where I was treated like a king.

On the Saturday morning their family maid served me the best breakfast I had ever eaten. When I was in England, eggs were rationed at one per person per week. If I was lucky the egg was bland but edible. Often, it would be rotten and I couldn't even look at it. At Mr Zaife's house I had four delicious scrambled eggs, a sausage, sliced tomatoes, chips, and a large glass of orange juice. I had never even imagined eating a meal like that.

Mr Zaife's 18-year-old daughter then took me out shopping and showed me the town. If first impressions counted for anything, Canada seemed like the greatest place in the world to live. All the people looked relaxed and worry-free, which made sense because food, and anything else you might ever want, seemed so plentiful.

On the way back from our excursion, we stopped at her father's store. There was a souvenir shop next door, where Mr Zaife bought a wallet for me and placed a ten-dollar bill in it as a parting gift. I still have that bill and treasure it as one of my prized possessions.

We left by train on Sunday night and, after dropping some children off in Montreal, we finally arrived in Toronto on Wednesday. I stayed there for a week before I was asked if I wanted to go to London, Ontario – a small city that is a two-hour drive from Toronto.

London's Jewish community had offered to absorb six boys and six girls. I was told I'd be placed in a retail fur business where I could learn the trade by serving an apprenticeship. I wasn't crazy about tool and die-making so this new option very much appealed to me. What I liked most about it was that I could follow in my father's footsteps and be a furrier just like he was.

It was an honourable route to take, though I must admit my real desire was to be able to continue my education and study music at university level. I always dreamed about being a composer, and felt that was my calling in life. No one, however, was willing to give financial support for this, so I just tried to make the most out of the opportunity that was presented to me.

Two members of London's Jewish community greeted me upon my arrival and gave me a place to stay for a week. They found work for me at Grafstein Furs, where Mr Grafstein gave me $10 per week to be his apprentice. With that and a $2-per-week stipend from the Jewish community I was able to pay for my room and board.

I also sold my accordion and violin in exchange for a set of drums, and joined a band that played at a local club. I made three to five times more money playing the drums three times a week than I earned in five or six days of working at the fur store. Occasionally, I would play at weddings and this was the most lucrative of all – where I could collect up to $50 in tips from guests.

I made enough money to eat well, own a decent wardrobe and even make one of my dreams come true. I had always wanted to own a car and eventually I saved enough to buy a used, yellow-and-black Ford. Life was better than I could have imagined and I was pleased that I had come to London.

I still dreamed, however, of emigrating to Israel, and when Israel obtained its independence in 1948 I badly wanted to go there and enlist in the army to help the country fight for its survival. But the appendix I had neglected in England came back to haunt me. After a painful attack it required emergency surgery, and by the time I had recovered the war was over. I also had to admit to myself that I was beginning to get quite comfortable in London so I decided to stay and continue the life I had begun.

At the age of twenty-two, after working for six years at Grafstein's, I asked Mr Grafstein for a $10 rise on my $50 per week salary. He refused, so I quit and opened up my own store. I was confident I could run my own business because I did all the same work as he did. The only difference was that he owned the store and had heaps of money whereas I was poor.

I started by renting a place across the street from Grafstein Furs. Naturally, that didn't please Mr Grafstein so he called the landlord and told her I didn't have any money and wouldn't be able to pay the rent. I couldn't convince her otherwise so I found another place two blocks away. This turned out to be for the best because the shop came with an upstairs apartment in which I could live.

I carved a niche for myself by specializing in remodelling and restoring old coats, and after doing some advertising, I got more work than I could handle.

Five years later, Mr Grafstein had to sell his business after becoming seriously ill. I bought his place and expanded my business to employ eight people. From then on the business just kept getting better and better.

I was spending 60 to 70 hours per week in the fur shop,

and playing in the band the rest of the time. I was working hard, but I was having fun. There was only one thing missing in my life – a family. No matter how much I enjoyed myself in Canada, I could not erase the past. My family had been taken away from me and that would never change. But at least I could start my own family. I was twenty-eight by this time and all my friends seemed to be married; several of them were already parents. With a stable foundation for a family – a house, a car and a good income – I decided that it was time to settle down. I began dating many young women, but couldn't find anyone special. Then I went on the trip of my life and met the woman of my dreams.

The fur season would typically be at its peak from October to March. At the end of March I would always take a holiday to recharge my batteries. In 1959 I decided I would go to Israel for a couple of weeks. I wanted to visit my friends who had emigrated there – and have the opportunity to meet their wives and see their children.

Unfortunately, just a couple of days prior to leaving I came down with a bad case of the flu. I thought about cancelling my trip, but decided to go despite my health. After all I had been through in life, I was not one to allow a little illness to get in my way.

Upon arrival in Israel it was raining very hard, with a terrible thunderstorm in progress. I took my luggage, passed through customs, and hired a cab to take me to a hotel. I made the mistake of not making any reservations, and it was during the Passover holiday period so it seemed almost every hotel room in the country was booked.

We drove around for more than two hours before we finally came upon a hotel in Tel Aviv where the clerk told me that that if I didn't mind sleeping in the lobby for a while there would be a vacancy the following morning. I accepted her offer without hesitating for a moment. I paid the taxi driver – giving him a good tip for his efforts. I checked in and fell asleep on a lobby couch at about 2.30 a.m.

When I woke up in the morning I felt feverish and my throat was very sore. I went up to my room and asked the woman at the front desk to send a doctor to see me. When the doctor arrived, my temperature was up to 104°F. He said I had caught an extremely nasty strain of flu. He gave me some antibiotics and said he'd be back to check on me the next day.

'It's a real bad illness you have,' he told me. 'I've just seen a woman die from it earlier in the week.'

I couldn't believe he told me that. It got me very worried. Fortunately, each day I got a little better and after four days I felt well enough to leave my room and eat dinner in the restaurant downstairs.

I sat at my table and ordered some cognac to drink before I ate my meal. At the table next to me were a man and a young woman in an Israeli military uniform. I remember that it was odd because they spoke Russian and not Hebrew. I wandered over and speaking mostly in English – because I didn't speak Hebrew and knew only a little Russian – I asked them why they were speaking Russian. The man spoke English, and told me that they immigrated to Israel from the Soviet Union after World War II and that they still used their native language a lot.

They invited me to sit down with them, and asked me where I was from and why I was in Israel. I told them I was from Canada and on holiday, but that I had lost the first four or five days of it because I was too ill to do anything but lie in bed. After we had dinner together, they invited me to go to the cinema with them and, although I still felt weak, I took them up on the offer.

Despite the language barrier, I really enjoyed my time with that young lady and wanted to get to know her better. Unfortunately, when the evening ended, all I knew was that her first name was Sonia, she was serving in the army and that she was from Haifa.

The next day was Friday so I booked a hotel in Haifa and took a cab up to the city. I explained to the cab driver that I was looking for a specific woman, and explained that she would probably be at the military camp closest to the city. Because it was Friday, I knew that she would get to go home at the end of the day for the Sabbath, and I wanted to offer her a ride. The driver took me to a nearby camp where we asked the guard if a woman named Sonia was there.

The guard contacted the compound and a few moments later a Sonia was driven by jeep to the front entrance. Unfortunately, this Sonia was about three times as large as the woman I was looking for. I thanked the guards for their help, and told the cab driver to leave and try another camp. Then, out of the corner of my eye, I saw the Sonia I had met walking out of the gate. I yelled at the driver to stop the car. In my broken Russian I asked her if she wanted a ride home, which she accepted.

As I dropped her off, I invited her for dinner at my hotel. She said she'd talk it over with her parents and get back to me. After conferring with them she accepted my invitation. When I picked her up she looked stunning, beautifully made up for a night out. We had dinner, and went out to a nightclub afterwards before I took her back to her parents' place.

The next day she called me to tell me she had two weeks off and could show me around Haifa that day. We had lunch and then we spent the rest of the day seeing the sights. We had a great time – so good that I asked her if she wanted to spend the rest of my holiday with me touring around the country. She accepted, as long as her father could come with us. I said that was fine and that we'd go the next day. I rented a car and we had a great time with what remained of my holiday.

It may seem strange judging by today's practices, but I was convinced she was the right woman for me. It didn't matter that we had barely met; I just knew somehow that we were meant to be, and the day before I was to leave Israel for Canada I asked her if she would marry me.

To my great joy she accepted my proposal, and I delayed my departure by two weeks so we could get married in Haifa. There wasn't much time to plan the event, but we managed to make all the arrangements and we had more than a hundred friends and family attend. It was a very bitter-sweet day for me. While one's wedding day is naturally a joyous occasion, it is also one to be shared with family. And while I was surrounded by so many of Sonia's relations no one was there from my family. That was extremely depressing.

None the less, as the evening progressed we had a great time, and excitedly went to Ashkelon in the south of the country for our honeymoon.

Then it was time for me to return to Canada. It was a tearful goodbye, but at least I knew Sonia would soon be joining me. Eight weeks later she arrived in Montreal, where I picked her up and drove her to London. It was such a brave thing for her to do. She was just eighteen yet she gave up all she had known in Israel to join me in Canada where she didn't know anything about the language or culture. All she came here with was a blind faith in our love.

Our relationship motivated me to work even harder so I could make her happy after she had sacrificed so much to be with me. And although I still was not rich by any stretch of the imagination, I decided to bring Sonia's mother and three younger siblings to Canada so that she could be with her family. (Her parents had separated, so her father stayed in Israel.)

At the same time, we began to start our own family, and over the following decade we had four children – three boys and a girl. I am proud that we were able to raise them in the wonderful country of Canada.

Words cannot express how happy I am that I chose to come to Canada. It was the best thing I have ever done. I have a lovely family here, and I have been able to live a productive life full of opportunity.

In 1998 I celebrated my 50th year in Canada. I have enjoyed 40 years of a terrific marriage, have had the privilege of seeing my children grow up with an education, and have experienced over 45 years of owning my own business.

Given everything that has happened to me – the fact that I miraculously escaped death as a young boy having witnessed nothing but pain and tragedy – I am pleased to say that because of my life here in Canada I will leave this earth a very happy man.

Epilogue

The close kinship I maintained with fellow survivors was one of the main sources of strength that enabled me to make it through the war. We were like family to each other and one of the joys of my life was seeing several of them survive. Many of those that endured are still alive today.

After all we had overcome during the war, it was most ironic and tragic when my closest friend Zybyszek died after we were liberated. A Soviet soldier shot him and I do not know any other details. I'm not sure whether he was just in the wrong place at the wrong time, or if he did something serious to provoke the soldier. Whatever the case, I was deeply saddened by his death and to this day I feel a sense of loss that he did not have the opportunity to find the joy in life that I have, and that our friendship never had the chance to make it into adulthood.

Romek, another of my closest friends in our gang, also didn't survive the war. One day we were washing and playing in the Vistula at a time when the water levels were dangerously high. One of our boys called for help as he was having problems staying afloat. Romek dived in to help him. The boy was able to grab a tree limb and get to safety, but Romek got caught in an undertow and drowned. His body wasn't discovered until the next day. The oppression we experienced hardened all of us, but Romek had somehow managed to remain the most polite, kindest boy in our group. His death was a severe blow to all of us.

Most of our group, however, did survive. Golec, the older boy Mrs Lodzia hid for a week, came to Canada and settled in Montreal. He became a successful businessman, got married, had five children, and now has several grandchildren. We were very excited for him when shortly after the war he found out that his twin brother had survived in hiding. Golec is still alive, but his brother died about 15 years ago.

The other two brothers in our group, Pavel and Zenek, had quite a story to tell when we met up again after the war. When the Warsaw uprising took place while I was in Saska Kepa, Pavel and Zenek were still in the city. In a display of outstanding courage, they fought with the Armia Krajowa against the Germans. Just before the war ended they were captured and taken to Germany, where they were liberated. In the Warsaw battles, they performed many heroic acts and were decorated with medals after the war. Unfortunately, they had to conceal their identity as Jews, and when their identity was eventually revealed, they were not treated as heroes any more, despite all they had done.

After the war they emmigrated to Israel. When their new country was attacked, soon after gaining independence, they fought valiantly in its defence, and soon after became high-ranking officers. Today, Pavel's sons continue the tradition of being officers in Israel's forces. Zenek also married and raised a family there. Unfortunately, he died of cancer in 1996. Pavel, who is now retired, still lives in Tel Aviv.

Many others in our gang also made it to Israel, including 'Bolus' – who also joined the Israeli military. As well, the Amchu man – who survived in his hole in the ground right up until the end of the war – found his way to Israel. He became a bus driver there before dying in the 1970s.

The friends who did not go to Israel are scattered throughout the world from Argentina to Australia. A few, however, such as Golec, live quite close to me. Irving, our main connection for Aryan papers, became a businessman in Niagara Falls, Ontario. He got married and has two brilliant children – an architect and a physicist. I also have good friends who chose to move to Detroit and Philadelphia in the United States.

My smuggling buddy Sevek moved to Toronto where he still lives with his family. Sevek aided me through so many difficult moments, including helping me carry my father's body from our upper-floor apartment. When we meet at weddings or bar mitzvahs, we fondly discuss both our families who lived in that dwelling. He lost his mother and sister in the ghetto while his father and brother suffered an unknown fate after crossing the border to Russia.

I do not know of the fate of many of the wonderful people who touched my life during the course of the war. I can only assume that the four men – Jankiel, Szlojme, Jacob and Aaron – died after leaving the ghetto. I did learn that Zlata never made it out and died when it was razed to the ground.

Perhaps most special of all during the war was Mrs Lodzia – the woman who hid me for almost a year and a half. I could never say enough about how much that wonderful person helped me. She lived life to the full each day and was willing to risk her life, and her children's, in order to save me. In reality, I was like a son to her and she a second mother to me.

I stayed in touch with the Lodzia family from the day I left Poland, sending parcels and money at Easter, Christmas and birthdays. Mrs Lodzia died in 1978 at the age of 73, following a long battle with cancer. Of her daughters only Irka remains alive today. The other, Marysia, was 56 when she too died of cancer. I still correspond with Irka, and I am touched when her children refer to me as Uncle Jankiel in their letters.

As for my children, I am extremely proud of them. Each has gone on to receive the university education I never had, and all are successful professionals in Toronto. Mark, the oldest, has an undergraduate degree in commerce and an MA in business administration. He works for a large Canadian retail company. Irv, the second oldest, is an electrical engineer working for a power company. Ed, the youngest boy, has an undergraduate degree in science and an MA in journalism. He now works in the field of corporate communications. Brenda, the youngest of the four, has just completed her MA in philosophy. Two of the boys – Irv and Ed – are already married. One of the greatest joys of my life took place earlier this year when I became a grandfather with the birth of Katheryn, Irv's daughter.

Sonia's family has also prospered since coming to Canada. Her mother Eva has just retired after owning a clothing shop in London for many years, and her brothers Neil and Bill and sister Marsha each moved to Toronto, got married, and now have families of their own.

As I reflect back on the events of my childhood, my many experiences have taught me above all just how precious life is. Surviving daily misery was an education in appreciation. I learned to savour the joy of simply breathing fresh air. Eating a good meal was like being in heaven.

I feel fortunate that I have gone on to lead a normal life in a great country. In fact, sometimes I find it difficult to believe I am the same person who experienced all the tragedies described in this book. When I think about all that I went through – and the emotional scars and the guilt that still remain – I realize how lucky I am. Many other survivors could not adjust and spent the rest of their lives unable to cope.

Still, there have been many times when it has been difficult to live with the horrors of my past. It is common for me to have terrifying nightmares of Germans chasing me, or that I'm trapped in a burning hiding-place.

I sometimes think about what would have happened had the Holocaust not happened. It is likely that my family would have branched out to hundreds of members. What they all could have achieved had they been given the chance will be unknown for ever. It is still very difficult for me to understand how I could not find even a single lost cousin.

I remember my sister Brenda had a wallet filled with photographs of my parents and the rest of us. What I would give for just one of those photos. I have only a few precious photos left – and they are in this book – most notable is a picture of Eli and I taken not long before his death. It sits prominently on our living room mantelpiece. Only in my memory can I now visualize my parents, my other brothers and my sister. I never had the joy of seeing them grow up, of seeing nieces and nephews being brought into the world.

The Holocaust should never have happened. I still find it hard to grasp how Germany – such a prominent nation – could have demonstrated such vicious behaviour.

In 1993 the 50th anniversary of the Warsaw ghetto uprising was celebrated in Poland. I had made plans to make the trip and see all my friends gathered there again. But in the end I couldn't bring myself to go. It would hurt too much. I can never go back to Poland. My memories of Warsaw are too sickening, filled with vivid memories of pain, sorrow and suffering. I feel nothing but hatred and bitterness towards the place. I couldn't even visit my parents' graves because the cemetery is gone – apartment buildings have been erected where the graveyard used to be.

Jews will probably never be able to live free and dignified lives in Poland. Anti-Semitism is still very much part of the national mindset there, as it is in many other countries. Even in the most tolerant countries such as Canada, Jew-hating still thrives. From the days of the Spanish Inquisition to the neo-Nazi movement of today, Jews have always paid a heavy price for their existence. The longer I live, the less sense it all makes to me. Why is the Jew always picked on and persecuted? Why is the Jew always the scapegoat?

It seems to me that because Jews were Hitler's target, no one raised an eyebrow. Had it been another race of people, I wonder whether the rest of the world would have rallied, intervened at an early stage and prevented the whole gigantic tragedy. During the war there was a boat with 1,000 Jews aboard that sailed the Atlantic; those on board hoped that the Americans or British would offer refuge. They were rejected and forced to return to Europe where they were murdered like all the other Jews. Neither Churchill, Roosevelt nor any of the other supposedly benevolent leaders offered help when it was needed.

But who is to say another Holocaust will not occur? Perhaps we still haven't learned the lesson – as we have seen recently in the Balkans and in Central Africa. If we are to prevent such a tragedy from happening again, those who lived through the horror must make others aware of what happened. The generations of the present and the future must know.

In light of such horror, it is not surprising that voluminous amounts have been written about the Holocaust. However, this will not last for ever. In less than a generation, there will be few, if any, people around who can provide first-hand accounts of what happened to them. I suspect mine will be among the last.

My friend Joe, the man who gave his daughter to Polish farmers and died after stabbing a German in the Umshlagplatz, had a maxim that he repeated to me to keep my spirits up as we confronted the anxiety of hiding in an attic. 'Where there is life there is hope,' he said, 'and where there is hope there is life.' One of the main reasons I survived the war was that I never relinquished my hope. And for the future, I must also remain hopeful. Perhaps one day the lessons of the Holocaust will truly be learned and humankind will be able to live in a world free from the cancer of bigotry.

December, 1999

Surviving the Nazis, Exile and Siberia

Edith Sekules

From Vienna to Estonia and finally to the United Kingdom, Edith Sekules tells her story of the consequences of being born Jewish in Vienna at the beginning of the century.

2000 176 pages

From Thessaloniki to Auschwitz and Back, 1926–1996

Erika Myriam Kounio Amariglio
Translated by Theresa Sundt

This is the story of Erika Kounio, deported in 1943 from Saloniki to the KZ Auschwitz, where she worked for two years as a scribe in the Gestapo office. It ends with her liberation, reunion with various members of her family, and her decision to continue to love and embrace life.

2000 256 pages

My Child is Back

Ursula Pawel

In *My Child is Back,* Ursula Pawel relates her experiences in Germany from her birth in 1926 to the start of a new life in the USA after the war. Her father was a Jew, her mother a Christian, but although their marriage shocked some relatives, such "mixed" marriages were not uncommon in the 1920s. Ursula had a happy early childhood, but with Hitler's rise to power, persecution of Jews (including "half-Jews" like Ursula) started immediately. Ursula's mother rejected all Nazi pressure to divorce "the Jew", and some of the non-Jewish relatives gave the family loyal support, but the parents finally recognized their mortal danger. It was, however, too late.

2000 192pp illus

VALLENTINE MITCHELL
Newbury House, 900 Eastern Avenue, Newbury Park, Ilford, Essex IG2 7HH
Tel: +44 (0)20 8599 8866 Fax: +44 (0)20 8599 0984 E-mail: info@frankcass.com
NORTH AMERICA
c/o ISBS, 5804 NE Hassalo Street, Portland, OR 97213 3644, USA
Tel: 1 800 944 6190 Fax: 503 280 8832 E-mail: cass@isbs.com
Website: www.vmbooks.com

Holocaust Literature
Schulz, Levi, Spiegelman and the Memory of the Offence
Gillian Banner
Foreword by **Colin Richmond**

Holocaust Literature provides an evaluation of the dynamics of memory in relation to representations of the Holocaust. It examines the compulsion to remember, the dilemmas of representation, and the relationship between memory, knowledge and belief in the works of Bruno Schulz, Primo Levi and Art Spiegelman. *Holocaust Literature* combines close readings of individual works, supported by a sound theoretical framework, with a consideration of the varieties of memory, and the particular problems of Holocaust memory. This approach reveals a 'hierarchy of remembrance' which exemplifies the changing nature of representations of Holocaust memory.

2000 184 pages 14 b/w illus
Parkes-Wiener Series on Jewish Studies

The Journal of Holocaust Education
Editors: **Jo Reilly** *(Executive), Institute of Contemporary History and The Wiener Library;* **David Cesarani,** *University of Southampton;* **Colin Richmond,** *Keele University*

Devoted to all aspects of interdisciplinary Holocaust education and research, the journal aims to reach a wider audience including scholars in Britain and overseas, teachers inside and outside the University sector, students, and the general reader interested in both the Jewish and the non-Jewish experience. At a time when the subject is taught in more universities and schools than ever before, *The Journal of Holocaust Education* is well placed to act as an important resource and as a forum for debate for all those interested in Holocaust education.
ISSN 1359-1371 Volume 9 2000
Three issues per year: Summer, Autumn, Winter

VALLENTINE MITCHELL
Newbury House, 900 Eastern Avenue, Newbury Park, Ilford, Essex IG2 7HH
Tel: +44 (0)20 8599 8866 Fax: +44 (0)20 8599 0984 E-mail: info@frankcass.com
NORTH AMERICA
c/o ISBS, 5804 NE Hassalo Street, Portland, OR 97213 3644, USA
Tel: 1 800 944 6190 Fax: 503 280 8832 E-mail cass@isbs.com
Website: www.vmbooks.com